Bridges

BRIDGES

United States Academia for First-Generation and International College Students

SHAWN M. HIGGINS, PH.D.

Art by Ian Lynam

BRIDGES

United States Academia for First-Generation and International College Students

SHAWN M. HIGGINS

NORTH
BROAD
PRESS

AN IMPRINT OF TEMPLE UNIVERSITY PRESS

PHILADELPHIA ROME TOKYO

North Broad Press is a joint publishing project between Temple University Press and Temple University Libraries, publishing works of scholarship, both new and reissued, from the Temple University community. All North Broad Press titles are peer reviewed and freely available online. More information is available at http://tupress.temple.edu/open-access/north-broad-press

Temple University Press
Philadelphia, Pennsylvania 19122
www.tupress.temple.edu

ISBN 9781439919859 (paperback); 9781439919866 (ebook)

To my teachers—the good, the bad, and the ones who brought donuts on final evaluation day.

To all those "underachieving" kids who repeated classes in summer school and are doing awesome things in their lives now.

To the university administrators who put quality of instruction over profit margins, who seek out ways to make precarious students and staff safe, who lead by example, and whose actions speak louder than their listserv emails.

To all the students without a mentor. If you don't have one, I would like to extend an offer: contact me. Ask me some questions, and I'll see if I can offer advice, wisdom, or support. Feel free to email me: shawn.higgins@tuj.temple.edu

TABLE OF CONTENTS

Acknowledgments ix

Who Is This Book For? xi

Why "Bridges"? xiii

For Students: Some Important Definitions xv

For Instructors: Some Important Considerations xix

Getting In 1

1. Accreditation and Types of Institutions 3

2. International United States College Campuses 7

3. Study Abroad in the United States 9

4. College Fairs 11

5. Outreach Services 13

6. Community Serving Colleges and Universities 15

    American Indian Tribally Controlled Colleges and Universities 15

    Alaska Native and Native Hawaiian-Serving Institutions 17

    First-Generation Forward Institutions 18

    Hispanic-Serving Institutions 22

    Historically Black Colleges and Universities 22

    Online Institutions 28

    Veteran-Serving Institutions 30

    Women's Colleges and Universities 33

7. College Rankings 37

8. Campus Visits 39

9. College Websites and Other Internet Resources 43

10. Applications 47

    Undergraduate School 47

    Graduate School 49

Getting Through 53

11. Common Challenges 55

    General Problem Solving 56

    Money 58

    Warning About Predatory Loans 61

    Getting Involved 61

    Time Management 62

    Dormmates/Roommates 63

    So Many Questions–Whom to Ask? 64

    Goal Setting 66

12. Academic Advising 67

13. Credentials, Majors, and Requirements 73

14. Instructors and Professors 77

    Job Titles and Pronouns 77

    Office Hours 79

Letters of Recommendation   80
15. *Diversity, Inclusion, and Equity*   83
16. *Rights and Responsibilities*   89
17. *More Quotes From the Field*   91
Appendix   97
18. *Twenty Academic Jargon Words You Might Need to Know*   99
19. *Grammar for Composition Resources and Review*   105
Components of a Sentence   107
Subjects   107
Prepositional Phrases   107
Verbs   108
Sentence Structure   109
Collective Nouns   109
Sentence Combining: Conjunctive Adverbs   110
Sentence Combining: Subordination   111
Sentence Combining: Run-on Sentences   113
Parallelism   114
Good Paragraphs   117
Topic Sentences   117
Supporting Sentences   118
Concluding Sentences   119
Transitions   120
Academic Paragraphs   122
Thesis Statements   123
Audience   125
Introduction Paragraphs   125
Body Paragraphs   126
Conclusion Paragraphs   127
20. *Academic Situations and Scripts*   129
In Emails   129
In the Classroom   131
In Office Hours   132
21. *Pop Culture Index*   135
Best African American Films   136
Best Asian American Films   137
Best International Feature Film Winners   138
Best Hispanic and Latinx American Films   139
The EGOT List   139
The Literary List   143
The Kennedy Center Honor List   144
The Kennedy Center Mark Twain Prize for American Humor   147
About the Author   148

ACKNOWLEDGMENTS

First, I want to thank the Bridge Program students at Temple University, Japan Campus—past, present, and future. Your dreams are so big, and you are working so hard to achieve them. This book is for you. I hope it's helpful.

Mary Rose Muccie, Annie Johnson, and Alicia Pucci of Temple University Libraries and Temple University Press were so wonderful to work with. Thank you for finding value in this project and for helping get this information to students around the world. I also want to thank my two anonymous readers who provided such useful suggestions and criticism. This manuscript is much stronger because of you.

Thank you to Bruce Stronach, Dean of Temple University, Japan Campus, as well as the Dean's cabinet, including Tom Dreves, Masamune Furukawa, Chie Kato, George Miller, Paul Raudkepp, and Miyuki Shoju, for making Temple University, Japan Campus a great place to teach, research, and grow.

Emiko Mizunuma, the Director of the Academic English Program and of the Undergraduate Bridge Program, has been a champion of mine ever since 2011 when I finished my master's program and came to teach in Japan. She is a hard-working visionary, and Temple University, Japan Campus is lucky to have her. I'm lucky to work with her.

Thank you to all of my colleagues in the Bridge Program: Karin Admiraal, Sarah Allen, Trevor Ballance, Kevin Buckley, Graham Christian, Hank Curtley, Dan Clapper, Jonathan Derr, Mark Diab, Adriana Estevez, Eric Firestone, Felipe Franchini, Shota Fujii, Paul Furfaro, Nick Giarratani, Teppei Hayashi, Kung-Cheen Howng, Sandy Ito, Jamil Karim, Luther Killebrew, Jiekai Liao, Thomas Meyer, Shayela Mian, Yuki Nakamura, Jill Okamoto, John Rajeski, Jonathan Richardson, Susana Sanchez, Kathy Schmitz, Tiffany Toeda, Adam Valerio, Matthew Williams, and Holly Woolbright. Rab Paterson and I worked closely together during short-session programs, and I am honored to call him a colleague and a friend. Jeff Hulihan of the Academic English Program has been a mentor here at TUJ since 2011, and I want to thank him for his wisdom and support. Mark Azzopardi gave me a great foundation from which to keep building as the first academic coordinator for the Bridge Program.

I would not be able to do my job of touching hearts and opening minds on my campus without the guidance and support of the following: Sunghee Ahn, Ada Angel, Jeremy Baba, Tom Boardman, Nicole Despres, Anais DiCroce, Glenn Davies, Hisako Deakin, Paul Gaspari, Tom Gurney, Yasuko Harada, Maki Hirono, Scott Tatsuro Inagaki, Masaki Kakizaki, Hana Kadosawa, Jeff Kingston, Ayako Kitaoka, Kanako Kunimatsu, Frank Lau, Ian Lynam, Zane Mackin, Andrew Merzenich, Motoko Mita-Hasegawa, Ajisa Mitsui, Mai Mitsui, Mariko Nagai, Kazuko Nemoto, Atsuko Nogawa, Tomo Norman, Ryoko Otani, Geo Otsu, Lee Roser, Tina Saunders, Norihisa Shimada, Takeki Shimamoto, Dariusz Skowronski, Mika Sumida, William Swinton, Shojiro Takemoto, Hanako Utahara, Danielle Vokal, May Watabe, Shinya Watanabe, and Jonathan Wu.

I also want to acknowledge and thank my former colleagues at the New Mexico Institute of Mining and Technology: Liza Apache, Gaby Benalil, Kip Carrico, Mary Dezember, Taylor Dotson, Doug Dunston, Susan Dunston, Benjamin Duval, Rosário Durão, Julie Ford, Paul Fuierer, David Grow, Janet Kieffer, Elizabeth Kramer-Simpson, Rafael Lara-Martinez, Yulia Mikhailova, Peter Phaiah, Lois Phillips, Jesse Priest, Alexander Prusin (RIP), Roland Rowe, and Steve Simpson.

I presented parts of the "For Instructors" section of this book at The American Studies Association of Korea's annual meeting at Korea University in 2019. I want to thank Russell Berman, Yoon-Young Choi, Barbara Demick, Jeannie Kim, Yangsoon Kim, Fred Lee, Tina Lee, Jungman Park, Jae Roe, Chenelle Seck, and Ka-eul Yoo for their conversation at this meeting.

I especially want to thank the people who contributed to sections throughout this book: Floyd Cheung, Shota Fujii, Teppei Hayashi, Patrick Lawrence, George Miller, Lata Murti, Mark Padoongpatt, Kristina Reardon, Eleanor Reeds, Otis Richardson, Sarajean Rossitto, Nitasha Sharma, Casey terHorst, and Caroline Kieu Linh Valverde. Also, a special shoutout to Ian Lynam for the awesome cover design work. Thank you all for your generosity!

Finally, I want to thank those closest to me. My best friend, Vince, made getting through my high school, community college, and undergraduate years fun, weird, and hilarious, and I've appreciated his support. My aunt, Jo Anne, has been a caring, loving, and thoughtful force in my life, and she has taken an interest in my intellectual and professional pursuits ever since I was a child. My father, Michael Patrick, has supported me in every decision I've made, even the tough ones like moving away from California to New York and then again out to Japan. More than anyone, I want to thank my wife, Mio, for all her love, sacrifice, and patience. I decided to get a doctorate degree because we thought high qualifications would help maintain our transnational relationship through transitions and visas over time. I couldn't have done any of this without her. To you, the reader—find someone to support you through your college years. It's a hard bridge to cross alone.

WHO IS THIS BOOK FOR?

This book is for students who are considering entering undergraduate or graduate school programs at a United States college or university. Some of the information in here might be useful for students entering specialty programs such as technical schools, law schools, executive programs, or medical schools. However, it does not directly discuss these programs.

This book is for two specific audiences: first-generation students and international students. If none of your close family members/caregivers/mentors went to college, or if you're an international student whose parents didn't go to college in the United States, you will need to do a lot of fact-finding research on your own. This book can help point you in the right direction.

There is some information that is easy to learn while you're applying for school or after you've entered, such as how to use your campus library or how to join student clubs. However, there is other information that I will call "legacy knowledge" that some students at your same stage of life already know because they have higher education mentors such as parents, relatives, or associates. Imagine it like this maze below:

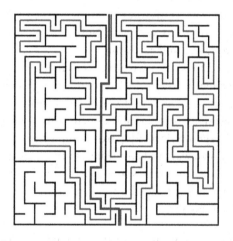

The red line represents first-generation "non-legacy" students, and the blue line represents "legacy" students. Both the red and blue lines begin and end at the same point. However, because of an early turn the red "non-legacy" student makes, their arrival at the exit point takes considerably more effort and time. It seems that the blue "legacy" student, by comparison, knows not to turn at that junction and to keep moving forward instead. The student traveling the blue line might have known the solution to the maze in advance and, therefore, wasn't intimidated by the maze's confusing turns. Perhaps the red student's longer trip through the maze was beautiful, interesting, and worthwhile in the end. However, if that blue path exists and if your goal is to exit this maze, which path would you rather take?

Hopefully, you too will learn all of the things "legacy" students know before you graduate. However, the time it takes on your path to reach the same destination as students with legacy knowledge might be frustratingly longer. As a first-generation undergraduate and graduate school student myself, I hope that this book helps uncover some of this legacy knowledge for you. I hope your journey through the maze has fewer turns and dead ends than my own did.

Let me explain a little about how I tried to write this book for you. I wanted this book to be simple to read. You might need a dictionary sometimes, but I tried to write things as clearly as possible. I also tried to avoid idioms, slang, and cultural references with which you might not be familiar. For English language learners, I hope those of you with a 475 or higher on the paper-based TOEFL test or with a 5.0 on the IELTS test will be able to read this without too many problems.

I also wanted this book to be accessible for visually impaired students using screen readers. Therefore, I left the formatting very simple. For example, instead of using text boxes and charts, I used tables and bulleted lists. Furthermore, I also avoided using many colors in consideration of colorblind users. I have strong protanopia, meaning I can only see about ten thousand shades of color while most other human eyes can see more than ten million. The result of these efforts is a boring-looking textbook. However, I hope that it's one of the easiest to read for people of all abilities.

This book is also shorter than many other college success texts. I didn't want to intimidate you with hundreds of pages of things you need to be or do in order to be a good college student. I wanted you to finish the whole book easily and to feel that satisfaction of accomplishment.

Unlike college success texts in retail stores or online marketplaces, this one is free and will remain so forever. I was very excited to work with North Broad Press on this book because this kind of information should be free and accessible.

Finally, I was also excited to write a Creative Commons-licensed textbook because they often include a "remix" element to them. I worked all through college as a DJ on the radio, in dance clubs, and at parties—I love a good remix. In a Creative Commons project, writers can "remix" the writing of others if we attribute them. Like a musical remix, when I remix something in this book, I take my favorite parts of someone else's work and add my own words to it, arrange it in my own way, and edit things to fit my purpose. For any other authors considering using my work in their remixes, please note that I did not copy and paste any of these other works directly into mine; I added my own grammatical changes, words, and stories. In this book, I remixed the following:

- Hall, Barbara and Elizabeth Wallace. *College ESL Writers: Applied Grammar and Composing Strategies for Success*. English Open Textbooks, 2018. (CC-BY-NC-SA)
- Jones, Peter, Debra Miles, and Narayan Gopalkrishnan. *Intercultural Learning: Critical Preparation for International Student Travel*. UTS ePress, 2018. (CC-BY-SA)
- Lamoreaux, Alise. *A Different Road to College: A Guide for Transitioning to College for Non-traditional Students*. Open Oregon Educational Resources, 2016. (CC-BY)
- University of Minnesota. *College Success*. University of Minnesota Libraries, 2015. (CC-BY-NC-SA)
- University of Texas at Arlington. *No Limits: Foundations and Strategies for College Success*. Mavs Open Press, 2018. (CC-BY)

WHY "BRIDGES"?

If you downloaded this book because you thought it was about architecture, structural engineering, or urban planning, I'm sorry. It's not. At least it was free, right?

This book talks about bridges as metaphors, or as clear ways to understand abstract concepts.

Imagine you're on one side of a river and you want to get across to the other side. No, you *need* to get across to the other side. You have a few options: you can try to walk through it if your feet touch the ground. You can try to swim across it. You can walk along the side of the river looking for a bridge to cross. Finally, if there's no bridge to cross, you can try to tether something to the other side of the river and build your own bridge to pull yourself across or to walk across.

Before you needed to get across that river, maybe you didn't care much about bridges. Bridges are just ways to get from one place to another—from San Francisco to Oakland, from Brooklyn to Manhattan. The bridge doesn't matter; it's the destination that you care about, right?

Well, this book focuses on bridges because they are important. Metaphorically, to get from high school to college, you need a bridge. If you're an international student, to move from your country's customs to those of the United States, you need a bridge. You need a bridge between the academic and the social aspects of college life. And if you can't find a bridge, you'll have to build one yourself.

Bridge-building is hard, whether it's literal or metaphorical bridges. The good news is that you don't have to build every metaphorical bridge yourself. In fact, many bridges are already in place and were built by experts. However, you will need to know where they are. Otherwise, if you can't find them, you will struggle unnecessarily all the way to your destination. You will have to build some. However, unlike a game where you have unlimited chances to try again, you only get limited shots at some metaphorical bridge-building. Therefore, instead of leaving you to try things on your own (like I had to, many times), I decided to write this book to show you where those bridges might be and how to build one if needed.

Throughout this book, I will try to refer to this metaphor. I hope it makes sense. If it doesn't (or if you just don't like it), just remember: being successful in college is about making connections, seeing relationships, solving problems, engaging actively, and figuring out how to get from "here" to "there." Find bridges where they already are; figure out how to make them when you need them.

FOR STUDENTS: SOME IMPORTANT DEFINITIONS

First, let's define "first-generation students" and "international students."

Being a "first-generation student" literally means you are the first person in your family to attend a college or university. If a college or scholarship application asks you this question, this is how they are probably defining the term.

However, this definition isn't always fair. For example, what if your father graduated from a university, but he has been out of your life since you were five years old? Technically, you would be at least a "second-generation student." Even so, if your father never gave you any advice about how to apply to college or told you any stories about his time on campus, you would feel like a "first-generation student," right? Similarly, what if you have an older sister who went to college? She's the same "generation" as you are biologically. Even if she helps you choose the best colleges to apply to, it seems strange that you would be "second-generation" at that point, right? Imagine if you had two younger siblings in that family. Would it make the youngest a "fourth-generation" student? I don't think so. In addition, some people might include extended family, such as aunts and uncles, as well as cousins in their definition. If your aunt graduated from a university but neither of your parents did, are you first-generation or second-generation? Maybe you're close with your aunt and she shares information with you, but maybe you're not. What if you had a neighbor who really helped coach you into college? That neighbor isn't your family, but you feel like a "second-generation student" with all the advice and knowledge they've given you. Do you see a theme emerging from these questions and scenarios? **Instead of the standard definition, I would like to define a "first-generation student" as someone who doesn't feel that they've ever had a higher education mentor and who does not have access to personal experiences connected to the type of college they will attend.**

If we use this definition for "first-generation student," then how might "international student" connect with it? What if you're from a country outside the United States and your family has steadily attended and graduated from universities in your home country for the last 150 years, but you're the first person in your family to attend college in the United States? What "generation" would you be? You've definitely had some "higher education mentors" among all of your educated family members, but none of them know what it's like to study in the United States. In this case, I would like to consider you a "first-generation student." But who qualifies as an "international student"?

Being an "international student" literally means you are attending a university in a foreign country using a student visa. If a college, scholarship, or financial aid application asks you this question, this is how they are probably defining the term.

However, this definition isn't always fair either. For example, what if you and your family moved to California when you were sixteen, you established residency by living in the state for more than a year and by not planning to return home, and then you applied to college? Your situation would be very different from other "international students." You would not be attending college on a student visa. You would pay in-state tuition as opposed to the very expensive tuition international students pay. You would have the ability to work while you attend school (depending on your family's visa status) while international students are restricted from most off-campus work. In many ways, you're not an "international student" because you don't have the same kinds of stress: your family is living with you, you've made the United

States your new "home" instead of just a place to temporarily study, and you don't have to worry about what happens when your visa expires. However, you still might feel like an "international student" in other important ways. Linguistically, religiously, culturally, socially, experientially, you might not feel like a "domestic" student. **Instead of the standard definition, I would like to define an "international student" as someone who has experience living in a foreign country, who calls more than one country "home," and who brings that experience and that transnational identity to a college campus.**

This book is for you, first-generation students and international students.

I considered adding the term "non-traditional students" to my focus, but I chose not to for a few reasons. Most importantly, I don't think the term "non-traditional" is very useful anymore. "Non-traditional student" historically has meant someone who does not attend college right after high school and who does not fit the profile of most undergraduate students. This might mean the student is financially independent, is employed already, is married, has children, is a military veteran, is a formerly incarcerated person, and more. First-generation students are all non-traditional students, but not all non-traditional students are first-generation students. Some non-traditional students are well prepared to apply to college because they have had mentors and know what university life is about. If "non-traditional student" includes someone whose parents both went to college but who took two years off after high school to backpack and sail around the world on their own money, then I don't think this book will be very necessary for them. But who knows? I hope it is, and I would be happy to know that this book helps as many people as possible.

I wrote this book because, for first-generation and international students especially, academia is confusing. Each college and university is different. Your school will have its own unique history, unique culture, and unique way of doing things. Similarly, every department is unique. Professors in your English department might teach, grade, and interact with students differently than professors in biology or professors in mechanical engineering. There is no way one book can imagine and explain all these differences. Instead, this book will serve as a guide to, an introduction to, and a welcome to the world of United States college and university life.

Inside, you will find facts and figures about this world of academia. You will also find personal narratives about this world, some my own and some from my colleagues and friends. Subsections include general explanations about general concepts and aspects of United States colleges and universities as well as questions for self-reflection and classroom discussion.

In this book, I use "college" to mean institutions where you study general topics and earn your first degrees. In my own experience, I graduated from Riverside City College in California where I took entry-level classes in many subjects such as English, mathematics, anthropology, geography, music, and more. You might also attend a "college" affiliated with a university, such as Barnard College in New York City. Barnard College has a partnership with Columbia University. Students at these two different schools can take classes at both campuses and even join in the other campus' clubs and events. However, the two schools have different requirements for admission, different financial aid processes, and different student experiences.

I use "university" to mean institutions where you can earn not only your first degrees but also professional and graduate degrees. Riverside City College has no bachelor's, master's, or doctorate degrees; Barnard College has master's degrees, but only through its partnership with

Columbia University. However, the University of California and the University of Connecticut do offer all levels of degrees from bachelor's through professional and graduate degrees.

This is not the most complete guide to United States colleges and universities. Instead, I wanted this to be concise and in language that is easy to understand for non-native English readers. The University of Minnesota Libraries Publishing has a free, very comprehensive digital title called *College Success* (2015) that includes sections on subjects such as listening strategies, note-taking, and preparing for tests that this book does not.

FOR INSTRUCTORS: SOME IMPORTANT CONSIDERATIONS

This book is meant to serve as a guide to and lead-in for discussions about the first-generation and international student experience. Many sections include data, narratives, general information, pertinent hyperlinks, or discussion questions on relevant topics. The discussion questions are both reflective and generative, meaning you could flip a classroom and ask students to prepare answers before class, or you could use them for in-class brainstorming and discussion.

Before using this book in your course, I would ask you to be reflective as well with some of the following questions helping to guide your syllabus planning:

- What educational experiences do you share with your students?
- Conversely, where do your own experiences greatly differ from those of your students?
- What was different when you were in school compared to the era in which your students are studying?
- Who are your students? What do their personal lives look like?
- What access do they have, and to what resources or information are they denied access?
- Who at your institution might not be welcoming of your particular students? Why? How can you help make them feel more welcome?

As a pedagogical preface for instructors, I would also ask you to consider this: don't be a brutish professor. The Oxford English Dictionary explains that to be a "brute" means to be an unintelligent, unreasoning, and rough person, something like an animal or a beast. Sometimes, "brute" is used synonymously with "barbarian" when characterizing someone who is rude, wild, and uncultured. Etymologically, "barbarian" identifies a "foreigner," or someone who does not share the language and culture of a host civilization. However, is someone necessarily rude just because they don't share a language or a culture? I say no, but I also say that they *can be* when barbarians are also brutes.

I've been a brutish barbarian. I've traveled to Belgium, the Dominican Republic, France, Germany, Taiwan, and Thailand without as much as a paper dictionary in hand because I expected that my English would get me through. To be fair, I wasn't the most brutish; I never yelled at shop workers for not understanding my English, and I never spoke English at a condescendingly slow pace expecting better results. However, in the Westvleteren Flemish region of Belgium, I did try to ask for an English menu *in English*, which was pretty brutish of me. In Berlin, I did try to ask a metro station attendant for directions in English, even though any simple travel guide easily provides that template sentence in German. In these moments, I didn't even perform the easiest of tasks; I didn't make the least effort possible. Instead, I made no effort. I simply showed up with my American passport and my clearly enunciated English and expected to be greeted, not only at the border crossing but also at hotels, at restaurants, in taxis, and in the culture at large. I was being a brute. Don't like the word "brute"? Okay, replace it with "asshole." You're the instructor or professor; you're already in the position of power. No need to be a "brute" in addition.

When teaching students unlike yourself or teaching abroad, there are "barbarian" pedagogical moves and then there are "brute" pedagogical moves. The barbarian type runs the gamut so that gaffes are hard to categorize. A simple example would be writing a South Korean student's name on the whiteboard using a red marker. They might inform you that you've just listed them as a deceased member of the class, and you will (or should) learn not to do that again in consideration of that student's culture. At least, that's what the clumsy yet innocent barbarian does. The brute, in comparison, looks at that South Korean student and tells them that their culture doesn't matter. The brute tells them that their classroom is an extension of the United States of America, and that in the United States of America, students need to learn not to take silly things like that so seriously. Honestly, they'll tell the student, they're tired of this generation's incessant focus on "microaggressions," whatever the hell that means! They'll tell the student that they need to learn to assimilate if they want to succeed. They'll say they can't be bothered to switch pens for each student's preference.

> "So, what, am I supposed to do your name in green and then only blue for students from the southern hemisphere and then make sure I don't use black for any students who might be offended by my correlation of a marker color with a term used for skin color?"

See how quickly this fictitious caricature of mine got out of hand? Instead of simply acknowledging the action, showing care for how the action affected someone, and making an effort to change future actions, the brute doubles down on ignorance, stubbornness, and violence.

Here are a few of the more notorious brute actions I would suggest instructors and professors consider:

• Don't make your students change their names to accommodate your untrained tongue. Ever. Don't pitch it like it's "cool" to have an English name in an English language classroom. Don't botch pronouncing their name all semester. Don't laugh through your own failure to say their name correctly and turn it into an uncomfortable mess for everyone, even if you're faux-condemning yourself with an "oh, I just can't seem to get this right!" kind of phrase. Instead, make the effort. Do some research. Watch a YouTube video or two on basic pronunciation in your students' native languages. "Jiang," "Xing," and "Zhang" are different. Figure it out. Ask the student for help if you're not getting it right, and don't get offended or turn apathetic when they don't feel like helping you. They've been through this before, and they're not hopeful that you'll do better. Work on it. And then, when you've got it down perfectly and you come to class and say their name and know that you nailed it perfectly, don't expect applause. You haven't done anything special; you've just put forward a decent amount of effort. Keep working on it for future students in future semesters. Each one of your students deserves your attention and effort.

• Don't make assumptions about students' preferred pronouns and their usage of pronouns for others. Make it a point to put your preferred pronouns at the top of your syllabus and to talk about them on the first day of class. Personally, I prefer that students use "Dr. Higgins" and "he/him/his." After announcing that, I invite students to share their preferred pronouns with me publicly during class or privately either in office hours or by email. I also make it clear that they can update me on their preferred pronouns as the semester progresses. When you do this, be sensitive to your non-native English speakers.

These students who might not conform to hegemonic gender identities get it especially rough because, when they confidently announce that they prefer one gendered pronoun to another, or when they use a pronoun in their writing that seems grammatically incorrect, the linguistic authority standing in front of the room might challenge them. Since they're still learning the language, their adoption of a non-conventional pronoun seems like an error more than a choice. Don't challenge them; let this one slide. If they are making a mistake, they will figure it out soon enough without your insistence. At least at that point, they will have realized it for themselves. That's much better than having their preferred identity or their cultural usage of pronouns stamped out by someone who holds all of the cards in a very uneven linguistic power dynamic.

• Whenever possible, ask your students what questions they want answered in your class, what kinds of authors they want to be introduced to, what kinds of narratives they want to read, what problems exist in their lives that they want to be equipped to fix. Even if the class is focused entirely on American history or American literature, your students might want certain topics covered that you would never think of adding to your syllabus. Do this instead of telling students which authors they need to know, which texts are the most important, and which issues are the most relevant today. If accommodating them doesn't distract from the course's overall learning outcomes, then why not?

• If you're teaching at a United States college or university abroad, don't try to make "Americans" out of your students. The United States university abroad should not be used as an assimilative tool of soft power. Don't expect that your students abroad act like students back home. Definitely don't grade them on the premise that they should. American students might feel comfortable cutting a professor off mid-sentence or boldly countering a half thought put forward by another student in class, but that's not the modus operandi of all students. Instead, figure out how you can bring out the best in your students without forcing those students to fit your mold of what a "good student" is or does. For example, you think students should "actively participate," and you're bummed that your non-American students are so quiet in class. You chalk it up (rather condescendingly) to some cultural weakness like "everyone in this country is so shy" or a flaw in "this country's way of educating young students." Instead of doing this, you might accept that there are other non-verbal, asynchronous ways students can participate. For example, having your whole class join an online chatroom eliminates many stressful barriers such as pronunciation anxiety, the difficulty of jumping into a conversation gracefully, or producing an accurate, complex, functioning sentence on the spot for some would-be participants. Unless those skills were the things you were specifically testing students on, why not let them participate and discuss your course's content via this medium? This is only one example of accommodating your students, each and every one. Think of others after you get to know your students on an individual basis. Your class, just like the United States of America, doesn't need to have a "love it or leave it" mindset. Instead, you can make it a truly welcoming, divergent, powerful, and productive space by bringing out the best in everyone involved.

Getting In

1. ACCREDITATION AND TYPES OF INSTITUTIONS

Before you enroll at a college or university, it is very important that you learn about its accreditation, or its professional standing as a degree-granting institution. If you're unfamiliar with 'for-profit' colleges, do a quick internet search for cases involving the University of Phoenix, DeVry University, ITT Technical Institute, or the Corinthian Colleges. There are three different types of schools in the United States.

REGIONALLY ACCREDITED SCHOOLS

Regionally accredited schools are typically non-profit colleges and universities for students seeking degrees. Regionally accredited schools must have a high percentage of full-time faculty and good library facilities. The classes offered at these schools must be taught by qualified professionals. The credits earned at a regionally accredited school can typically transfer to other regionally accredited schools. Regional accreditation organizations include:

1. The Higher Learning Commission, formerly part of the North Central Association of Colleges and Schools, which accredits institutions in Arkansas, Arizona, Colorado, Iowa, Illinois, Indiana, Kansas, Michigan, Minnesota, Missouri, North Dakota, Nebraska, New Mexico, Ohio, Oklahoma, South Dakota, Wisconsin, West Virginia, and Wyoming.

2. The Middle States Commission on Higher Education, which accredits schools in Delaware, the District of Columbia, Maryland, New Jersey, New York, Pennsylvania, Puerto Rico, and the U.S. Virgin Islands.

3. The New England Commission of Higher Education, which accredits institutions in Connecticut, Maine, Massachusetts, New Hampshire, Rhode Island, and Vermont.

4. The Northwest Commission on Colleges and Universities, which accredits institutions in Alaska, Idaho, Montana, Nevada, Oregon, Utah, and Washington.

5. The Southern Association of Colleges and Schools, which accredits schools in Alabama, Florida, Georgia, Kentucky, Louisiana, Mississippi, North Carolina, South Carolina, Tennessee, Texas, and Virginia.

6. The Western Association of Schools and Colleges, which accredits schools in California, Hawaii, and the Pacific.

NATIONALLY ACCREDITED SCHOOLS

If a school is only nationally accredited, it might be a for-profit school such as a vocational, career, or technical college that grants certificates. Even though "nationally" sounds more powerful, most degree-seeking students will want to attend schools that are "regionally" accredited. Schools that are only nationally accredited might not have many full-time faculty members or good library facilities. The instructors at these schools may not have the highest degrees in their fields or competency in the subjects they teach. The credits earned at these schools may not transfer to other institutions.

UNACCREDITED SCHOOLS	Some schools never receive accreditation of any kind, and others lose their previous accreditation and become "unaccredited." Schools can lose accreditation when they close, merge with another institution, don't apply for accreditation renewal, or don't meet the standards of the accreditation review. The United States Department of Education does not decide which schools are accredited and which are not. Instead, regional and national accrediting organizations review colleges and universities and report their evaluations to the Unites States Department of Education.

The Council for Higher Education Accreditation has a searchable database of schools and their accreditation type. Choose the country, state, and maybe city of the school you're searching for, and choose "Any Accreditor," but don't type the name of the school in the search bar for "Institution." The official name of the university might be different than what you think. Then, search through the results you get to find the school you're thinking about.

Next, you should consider the type of institution in which you want to enroll. Each type offers a completely different experience in terms of the education style, social life, and alumni relations. Beyond the generic terms "college" or "university," here are some types to consider.

COMMUNITY COLLEGES	Sometimes also called "city colleges," these institutes offer education that follows high school and helps students earn certificates and associate degrees. Students who graduate from community colleges often can transfer, if they wish, to a four-year college or university to complete a bachelor's degree. Historically, community colleges were also called "junior colleges." However, in recent years, the term "junior college" has been used more frequently for private two-year institutions.

LIBERAL ARTS SCHOOLS	Liberal arts schools have smaller enrollments, emphasize instructor-student interactions, rely very little on teaching assistants, and are typically residential schools, meaning many students live in dorms for their first few years.

"PARTY SCHOOLS"	Like the term or not, some colleges and universities in the United States are more well known for partying, drugs, and alcohol than others. Popular publications such as *Playboy* and *The Princeton Review* publish annual rankings of "party schools," sometimes against the wishes of school administrators. As a prospective student, you should decide whether you want to be associated with an institution with this reputation or not. Many wonderful research universities such as the University of Wisconsin, the University of Texas at Austin, the University of Colorado Boulder, the University of Virginia, and Syracuse University have topped these lists in recent years.

"R-1 UNIVERSITIES" R-1 schools, or research universities at the highest level, focus primarily on the research projects of their professors and graduate students. These universities rely heavily on the work of teaching assistants, graduate assistants, and laboratory assistants to teach classes and meet with students. Students at these institutions might get to take classes with some of the world's leading researchers and experts. However, these classes could be very large, and students may not have much individual time with these professors and researchers. The only undergraduate-focused college typically on this list is Dartmouth College.

TECHNOLOGICAL INSTITUTES These colleges and universities are focused primarily on science, technology, engineering, and mathematics (STEM), with a few including arts (STEAM). The faculty members of these institutions are often working on research projects tied to governmental and private-sector funding.

VOCATIONAL INSTITUTES These schools are typically two-year colleges that prepare students to enter a specific career after receiving an associate degree. Some of these institutes offer classes that can transfer to a four-year university.

2. INTERNATIONAL UNITED STATES COLLEGE CAMPUSES

Did you know?

- The United States has seventy-seven international campuses, which is the largest number in the world. Other top exporters of international campuses include the United Kingdom (thirty-eight), France (twenty-eight), Russia (twenty-one), and Australia (fourteen).
- China and the United Arab Emirates host the largest numbers of international campuses with thirty-two each. Other top importers of international campuses include Singapore (twelve), Malaysia (twelve), and Qatar (eleven).
- In total, there are thirty-four countries that together host 250 international campuses.
- As the Cross-Border Education Research Team's data shows, international campuses are frequently opening and frequently closing! On the one hand, there might be a new international campus opening soon in your country. On the other hand, make sure the university you are thinking of attending is still accepting students and that it's not closed!

A degree from a United States college or university is a powerful thing. You can take that degree anywhere in the world and use it to introduce yourself. Graduating from a United States college or university requires certain personal and professional characteristics. These characteristics include being persistent, creative, flexible, goal-driven, independent, analytical, and more. Everyone knows from Hollywood films that students at United States colleges and universities love to party and have a good time. However, when assignments and exams get serious, these students also know how to work hard and get things done. United States middle school and high school courses might not compare well to the effective educational programs in other countries. Nevertheless, graduating from a United States college or university is no easy task; it's a major accomplishment.

If you don't live in the United States, leaving your home and family to go study abroad might be a scary thought for several reasons. You might be worried about the crime rate in the United States and the acts of terrorism carried out by armed gunmen. Your family might not be able to afford the high cost of tuition and living expenses. You might not want to leave your family, your friends, and your environment for that long of a time. In any of these cases, you could consider studying at a United States college or university located in a country closer to yours or even in your home country. According to the Cross-Border Education Research Team, colleges and universities from the United States have campuses in Australia, Austria, Canada, China, Croatia, Ecuador, England, France, Germany, Ghana, Greece, Hong Kong, Hungary, Israel, Italy, Japan, Mexico, The Netherlands, Nicaragua, Panama, Poland, Qatar, Russia, Rwanda, Saint Lucia, Singapore, Slovakia, South Korea, Spain, Switzerland, Thailand, and the United Arab Emirates. With campuses across the world, find one closer to home if that makes the decision easier.

If you're a United States college student who wants to study in another country, international campuses might also be a good choice for you. Some students are concerned about the quality of education or the name recognition of foreign universities and would be more comfortable studying at a familiar United States university. If you would like to travel abroad and gain life experience but also work toward completing your degree from a United States university, consider enrolling in an international campus, such as Temple University's Japan campus where I work. Some institutional bridges span wide distances. Dare to cross into new territories? (See? The metaphor kind of works).

Self-Reflection/Discussion Questions:

1. What is your impression of United States colleges and universities? What gave you this image?
2. What preparation do you need to do to be accepted to a United States college or university?
3. What is the biggest thing stopping you from studying at a United States college or university? Is this something you can change/overcome? If so, how?
4. Do you think graduating from a United States college or university would offer something different from graduating from a university in your home country? Why or why not?
5. Do you have a dream United States college or university? If so, which one and why?

3. STUDY ABROAD IN THE UNITED STATES

Quotes from the field:

"Study abroad is more than just taking classes and earning credits. It's about immersing yourself in a different culture. It's not only learning about others but also about yourself and your own culture and country. 'Home' will be different when you return because you will have been changed by your study abroad experience. It is my hope that students will take some time to reflect on what they have gone through. Then, they can figure out how they will apply their knowledge and experience to their future steps. There's so much more to be learned outside of the classroom."

—Teppei Hayashi
Study Abroad Coordinator, Temple University, Japan Campus

Did you know?

- Since 2015, there have been more than one million enrolled international students in United States colleges and universities each year. International students equal 5% of the total number of college and university students in the United States.
- The leading countries of origin for international college and university students in the United States are China (33%), India (18%), South Korea (5%), Saudi Arabia (4%), and Canada (2%).
- The United States universities with the highest numbers of international students are New York University, the University of Southern California, Northeastern University, Columbia University, and Arizona State University–Tempe.
- States with the highest numbers of international students include California, New York, Texas, Massachusetts, Illinois, and Pennsylvania.
- States with the fewest numbers of international students include Alaska, Maine, Montana, Vermont, and Wyoming.
- According to the Institute for International Education, the fields of study with the most international students in the United States are engineering, business and management, and math and computer sciences.

Not everyone is able to study abroad. It's expensive, it takes you away from your home and your family, and it comes with difficulties that can affect your personal life. I studied Latin in high school, and I would have loved to study abroad in Italy. I never got the chance. However, if I had known about the wonderful experiences that study abroad offers when I was a high school student, I might have brought the subject up with my dad and tried to find a way to make it happen.

Some study abroad opportunities might be more comfortable than others. If you live in Rochester, New York, and if you're an English speaker, studying abroad in Toronto, Canada, might be comfortable: the physical distance is short, and the language is the same. Just a few hours east from Toronto, however, is Montreal, where people not only speak English but also French. Studying abroad here would present a few more challenges. Yes, challenges, but you could also consider them opportunities instead. In this case, it is a strong opportunity to learn Canadian French with the ability to drive home in a short amount of time. Similarly, if you live in California, Arizona, New Mexico, or Texas, you could study abroad in Mexico with the same challenges/opportunities. Any time you cross an ocean, things become a bit more intimidating; you have to fly home, and flights can get canceled and can be very expensive during certain seasons. Unless you live in Canada or Mexico, studying abroad in the United States is a major commitment to pursue opportunities and to take on challenges.

Since 2017, the number of new international enrollments in the United States has been dropping. Changes in United States visa policy, the perception of the United States as "unwelcoming" to foreigners, and President Donald Trump's trade war with China are all factors in this decline.

International students pay more than domestic students do. Therefore, United States universities are ready and excited to admit students from abroad. Of course, having a diverse student population is nice for concepts like "embracing diversity" and "creating an environment of global leaders." However, the economic reality is that international students' tuition payments help keep in-state tuition charges down and help fund the university's operations. This is particularly true for large state universities that offer doctoral study programs such as the schools I attended—the University of California system and the University of Connecticut.

International students are an important part of the United States' economy. Studies done by NAFSA: Association of International Educators and by Studyportals estimate that these students have put $39–57 billion dollars into the national economy over the past ten years. This bridge toll admitting people into United States universities charges different rates for students based on where they're from. Did you ever stop to consider who pays more to keep certain bridges maintained and functional? (Okay, this metaphor got stretched a bit, but . . . it still makes sense, right)?

Self-Reflection/Discussion Questions:

1. Would you prefer to study at a university with a small or a large international student population? Why?
2. Are you interested in meeting people from any particular country around the world? If so, where and why?
3. Do you think international students should pay the same amount of tuition as domestic students? If not, should they pay more or less? Why?

4. COLLEGE FAIRS

Quotes from the field:

"I arrive at the St. Maur College Fair in Yokohama super relaxed. I'm confident because I have simple reading materials on subjects such as transfer credits, and I have the best swag to pass out to students, including candies, pens, and even a Kindle door prize. Best of all, I am excited to spend time with my colleagues and friends at the fair. My goal is to answer questions and promote awareness of our university brand. Luckily, many attendees already have a friend or a family member who went to our university. Instead of trying to sell our school aggressively, I talk to students about their favorite sports, future goals, and Netflix movies to watch. I want to let them know that our school is a chill community to join."

—Otis Richardson
Admissions Counselor, Temple University, Japan Campus

How do you pick which university is right for you? Maybe your parents went to a certain university, and so you think you might want to go there too. Maybe there is a nice university near where you live, and you think it would be convenient and logical to go there. Maybe you have a famous university in mind because you think going to that university will give you access to a successful career and happy life. But still, how do you pick which one? You can apply to many, but you can only choose one in the end.

One thing that may help you choose is a college fair. College fairs happen at big locations such as hotel meeting rooms, convention centers, or perhaps on specific university campuses. Representatives from colleges come to these fairs to meet potential applicants, to talk to you about campus life, and to explain the requirements for admission.

College fairs should be free and open to the public; do not attend a college fair with an entrance fee. You might need to register in advance through an organization's website, but there should not be any charge to attend (except perhaps for parking costs at the hotel/convention center).

For international students, meeting with these representatives gives you a good chance to ask about TOEFL or IELTS requirements as well as necessary financial forms for your application. You can ask these representatives if scholarships or financial aid are available for international students. The National Association for College Admission Counseling suggests that international students ask the following questions at the fair:

1. What percentage of this university's students are international?
2. From which countries do international students most commonly come?
3. How does this university support international students? For example, what if I get a serious sickness? What if I'm having a hard time culturally, socially, or emotionally?
4. Is acceptance into certain degree programs more competitive or more difficult for international students?
5. How do international students interact with American students on this campus?

6. What housing options are there for international students?
7. Do the dining options on campus consider international students? For example, are there vegetarian options? Kosher options? Halal options?
8. How easy it for international students to do things by themselves on weekends? Do international students need driver's licenses and cars?
9. How close is campus to the nearest international airport?
10. Can you share any recent success stories of international students on this campus?
11. Can you connect me with recent alumni or current students from my country so I can learn more about their experiences?

Meeting with an admissions counselor at a college fair is just like finding someone across a river who's willing to throw you a rope to help you get to the other side. You just need to make the effort to go to the river's edge and scream for help. Someone is waiting on the other side to help you get across.

Self-Reflection/Discussion Questions:

1. Have you ever been to any other kind of "fair" at a large gathering area, such as a wedding fair, a job fair, or a trade show? If so, what kind?
2. Would you be nervous about meeting with college representatives at a fair? If so, why?

5. OUTREACH SERVICES

If you agree with any of the following statements, then you might benefit from student outreach services:

- I don't have a clear goal after high school.
- I don't have a clear career goal.
- I don't know how I will pay for college.
- I don't have a good sense of which university classes I should take to reach my goals.
- I don't know the process to register for classes.
- I don't know which office on campus to talk to if I have general questions.
- I don't know how this school works with non-traditional students, especially veteran students.

Even if you have an idea for your personal goals, your academic goals, and your career goals, do you know how to achieve those goals? If getting into and then through college are two steps toward achieving those goals, and if you don't know much about United States academia, then those first two steps might be difficult ones. For first-generation students, students from underrepresented populations, international students, non-traditional students, veteran students, or students who for one reason or another are simply not informed about academia, student outreach services can help.

Many colleges and universities have dedicated student outreach services that provide advising, support, programs, and connection opportunities. These schools will speak with young students (as young as fourth grade elementary school) about plans of attending college. Student outreach services can help you schedule a campus visit, think about how best to fill out your college application, and answer any other questions you might have about how to reach your goals.

The government offers one type of student outreach program. Upward Bound is a federal program of the United States Department of Education. This program's goals are to help high school students enter and then successfully graduate from college. The students this program helps come from low-income families in which neither parent has a bachelor's degree. Upward Bound can also benefit English language-learning students, students from underrepresented groups in higher education, students with disabilities, students who are homeless, students who are in foster care, and other disconnected students. The program's website lists services provided such as tutoring, counseling, mentoring, cultural enrichment, and work-study programs. All Upward Bound projects *must* help students in the areas of mathematics, laboratory science, writing (composition), literature, and foreign language study.

Upward Bound provides programs in every state as well as the District of Columbia (Washington, DC), the Federated States of Micronesia, Guam, the Marshall Islands, Puerto Rico, and Palau. However, not every state gets the same amount of support, and not every college or university will have an Upward Bound program. For example, Rhode Island only has one Upward Bound program, which is hosted by Rhode Island College. However, Puerto Rico has thirteen Upward Bound programs hosted by nine different colleges and universities. Meanwhile, California has 145 Upward Bound programs hosted by educational corporations, community colleges, and small and large public and private universities.

For the 2018–2019 school year, Upward Bound programs were offered by 967 colleges and universities across the country. These programs benefited over 70,000 students with more than $355,000,000 in support. The number of programs offered and amount of funding provided has been steadily increasing over the last ten years.

Another specific type of outreach program is the "enrichment program." These programs can cost thousands of dollars, and participating in one does not guarantee that you will later successfully be accepted to the university of your choice. However, if you have access to financial resources, then you could greatly take advantage of the experiences offered by enrichment programs. For example, Summer Discovery is a pre-college academic enrichment program in which students live on a college campus, explore university towns, and are taught by university instructors during the summer months. Middle school programs have partnerships with the University of California, Los Angeles; the University of Colorado Boulder; and Georgetown University. High school programs have partnerships with Cambridge University (UK); City University (UK); the University of California, Los Angeles; the University of California, Santa Barbara; the University of Colorado Boulder; Georgetown University; Johns Hopkins University; the University of Michigan; the University of Miami; Pace University; the University of Pennsylvania; the University of Texas at Austin; and Yale-NUS College (Singapore). Some partial scholarships are available, but students should still expect to pay fees of a few thousand dollars.

It feels nice to join a university if its staff have clearly already built and maintained a bridge for you to cross over, doesn't it? Would you want to try to cross one that was dangerous and not taken care of?

Self-Reflection/Discussion Questions:

1. Do you already have a career goal? If so, what is it?
2. Do you already know the types of classes you will need to take to reach that goal? If so, what are they?
3. Do you think the government should provide special services to help children from low-income families get into college? Why or why not?

6. COMMUNITY SERVING COLLEGES AND UNIVERSITIES

As is explained in more detail in the "For Students: Some Important Definitions" section earlier in this book, a "college" is typically a two- or four-year institution where you study at the undergraduate level. A "university" is a four-year institution that offers both undergraduate and graduate level courses. In addition, there are many different types of colleges and universities in the United States.

Some colleges and universities have histories in serving particular populations such as women, religious groups, and African Americans. Others are now working toward supporting specific growing and/or struggling student populations. As a student, you might want to study at a college or university that has a rich history, diverse curriculum, and faculty members from a historically underrepresented population. You also might want to attend a school that makes an extra effort to support students like yourself. Consider the lists below if you fall into any of these categories. Check out their websites; each school's name links to their homepage.

American Indian Tribally Controlled Colleges and Universities

The Navajo nation created the first tribally controlled college in 1968 with Navajo Community College (now called Diné College). In December 2011, President Barack Obama signed Executive Order 13592 with the goal of improving American Indian and Alaska Native educational opportunities through strengthening tribally controlled colleges and universities. Many of these institutions are located in the poorest parts of the Midwest and Southwest in very rural and remote areas. Tribally controlled colleges and universities are important not only for American Indian communities but for the overall preservation and fostering of American Indian cultures, languages, and traditions. Any student interested in strengthening tribal nations and learning in an environment mixed with Native cultures and traditions might consider applying to one of these institutions.

STATE	COLLEGE OR UNIVERSITY
Alaska	Ilisagvik College
Arizona	Diné College
Arizona	Tohono O'odham Community College
Kansas	Haskell Indian Nations University
Michigan	Bay Mills Community College
Michigan	Keweenaw Bay Ojibwa Community College
Michigan	Saginaw Chippewa Tribal College

STATE	COLLEGE OR UNIVERSITY
Minnesota	Fond du Lac Tribal and Community College
Minnesota	Leech Lake Tribal College
Minnesota	Red Lake Nation College
Minnesota	White Earth Tribal and Community College
Montana	Aaniiih Nakoda College
Montana	Blackfeet Community College
Montana	Chief Dull Knife College
Montana	Fort Peck Community College
Montana	Little Big Horn College
Montana	Salish Kootenai College
Montana	Stone Child College
Nebraska	Little Priest Tribal College
Nebraska	Nebraska Indian Community College
New Mexico	Institute of American Indian Arts
New Mexico	Navajo Technical University
New Mexico	Southwestern Indian Polytechnic Institute
North Dakota	Cankdeska Cikana Community College
North Dakota	Nueta Hidatsa Sahnish College
North Dakota	Sitting Bull College
North Dakota	Turtle Mountain Community College
North Dakota	United Tribes Technical College

STATE	COLLEGE OR UNIVERSITY
North Carolina	University of North Carolina at Pembroke
Oklahoma	Bacone College
Oklahoma	College of the Muscogee Nation
Oklahoma	Pawnee Nation College
South Dakota	Oglala Lakota College
South Dakota	Sinte Gleska University
South Dakota	Sisseton Wahpeton College
Washington	Northwest Indian College
Wisconsin	College of Menominee Nation
Wisconsin	Lac Courte Oreilles Ojibwa College

Alaska Native and Native Hawaiian-Serving Institutions

These institutions can receive grants and related assistance to improve and expand their capacity to serve Alaska Natives and Native Hawaiians. An Alaska Native-serving institution must have an undergraduate enrollment that is at least 20% Alaska Native students. A Native Hawaiian-serving institution must have an undergraduate enrollment that is at least 10% Native Hawaiian students. Please note that the correct punctuation and pronunciation of the state of Hawaii is "Hawai'i." In organizing this list, I decided to use the simplified spelling of Hawaii for general searching purposes.

STATE	COLLEGE OR UNIVERSITY
Alaska	Alaska Pacific University
Alaska	Ilisagvik College
Alaska	University of Alaska Fairbanks, Interior Alaska Campus
Hawaii	Chaminade University of Honolulu

State	College or University
Hawaii	University of Hawai'i, Hawai'i Community College
Hawaii	University of Hawai'i, Honolulu Community College
Hawaii	University of Hawai'i, Kapi'olani Community College
Hawaii	University of Hawai'i, Kaua'i Community College
Hawaii	University of Hawai'i, Leeward Community College
Hawaii	University of Hawai'i, Maui College
Hawaii	University of Hawai'i at West O'ahu
Hawaii	University of Hawai'i, Windward Community College

First-Generation Forward Institutions

These institutions were awarded the designation "First-Generation Forward" by the Center for First-Generation Student Success, an initiative of the NASPA and The Suder Foundation. To be eligible, these institutions need to be accredited, be a member of NASPA, secure senior leadership support and commitment to participation, designate a minimum of two employees to serve as representatives, and commit to fulfilling the requirements of the program. These requirements include a series of training and educational seminars on how best to support first-generation students.

State	College or University
Alabama	Alabama State University
Alabama	Auburn University
Alaska	University of Alaska Fairbanks
Arkansas	Arkansas Tech University
Arkansas	NorthWest Arkansas Community College
Arkansas	University of Arkansas, Fayetteville
California	California State University, Channel Islands

STATE	COLLEGE OR UNIVERSITY
California	California State University, Sacramento
California	Loyola Marymount University
California	Marymount California University
California	University of California, Riverside
California	University of California, Santa Barbara
California	University of San Francisco
Connecticut	University of Bridgeport
Connecticut	University of Connecticut
District of Columbia	American University
Florida	The University of Tampa
Florida	University of Central Florida
Georgia	Georgia Southwestern State University
Georgia	Piedmont College
Hawaii	University of Hawai'i at Mānoa
Idaho	Boise State University
Illinois	DePaul University
Illinois	School of the Art Institute of Chicago
Illinois	Southern Illinois University, Carbondale
Indiana	Indiana University–Purdue University Indianapolis
Kentucky	Eastern Kentucky University
Kentucky	Kentucky Wesleyan College

STATE	COLLEGE OR UNIVERSITY
Louisiana	Grambling State University
Maryland	Carroll Community College
Maryland	St. Mary's College of Maryland
Maryland	University of Maryland, College Park
Massachusetts	Boston College
Massachusetts	Mount Holyoke College
Massachusetts	Simmons University
Massachusetts	University of Massachusetts Boston
Massachusetts	Worcester Polytechnic Institute
Michigan	Lake Superior State University
Michigan	Michigan Technological University
Michigan	University of Michigan–Dearborn
Minnesota	Carleton College
Mississippi	University of Mississippi
Missouri	Missouri State University
Missouri	University of Missouri–Kansas City
Nevada	University of Nevada, Reno
New Jersey	Monmouth University
New Jersey	Rutgers University, Camden
New Jersey	Saint Peter's University
New York	Cornell University

STATE	COLLEGE OR UNIVERSITY
New York	Nazareth College of Rochester
New York	The New School
North Carolina	North Carolina Agricultural and Technical State University
North Carolina	North Carolina Central University
North Carolina	University of North Carolina, Greensboro
Ohio	Cuyahoga Community College
Ohio	The Ohio State University
Oklahoma	Tulsa Community College
Oregon	Portland Community College
Pennsylvania	Allegheny College
Pennsylvania	Lafayette College
Pennsylvania	Shippensburg University
South Carolina	Presbyterian College
South Carolina	Winthrop University
Tennessee	Tusculum University
Texas	Angelo State University
Texas	Midwestern State University
Texas	Texas A&M University
Texas	Texas Lutheran University
Texas	Texas State University
Texas	The University of Texas at El Paso

STATE	COLLEGE OR UNIVERSITY
Utah	Salt Lake Community College
Vermont	Champlain College
Virginia	Virginia Polytechnic Institute and State University
Washington	Seattle University
Washington	University of Washington, Tacoma
Wisconsin	Madison Area Technical College
Wyoming	University of Wyoming

Hispanic-Serving Institutions

A Hispanic-Serving Institution (HSI) is an accredited and degree-granting institution of higher education with 25% or more of its full-time undergraduates identifying as Hispanic. In 2018–2019, there were 539 HSIs located in twenty-seven states, the District of Columbia, and Puerto Rico. Only 17% of all institutions of higher education in the United States met the requirements to be called an HSI. The states with the most HSIs include California (176), Texas (96), Puerto Rico (60), New York (34), Florida (29), Illinois (25), and New Mexico (24). Of all HSIs, 43% were public two-year colleges, 28% were private four-year colleges, and 26% were public four-year colleges. The remaining 3% were private two-year colleges. For more information on HSIs, visit the Excelencia in Education website or the Institutional Service home page of the Office of Postsecondary Education under the United States Department of Education.

Historically Black Colleges and Universities

The Higher Education Act of 1965 defines a historically Black college or university (HBCU) as an institution "established prior to 1964, whose principal mission was, and is, the education of Black Americans, and that is accredited by a nationally recognized accrediting agency or association determined by the Secretary [of Education] to be a reliable authority as to the quality of training offered or is, according to such an agency or association, making reasonable progress toward accreditation." Before 1964, Black Americans were not allowed to study at a majority of higher institutions of learning in the United States. Most of these institutions are in the South and the Midwest. Today, anyone can attend an HBCU, not just Black students. Some of these HBCUs, including Howard University, Spelman College, Xavier University of Louisiana, Hampton University, and Morehouse College, are highly competitive and have graduated very successful, famous alumni.

STATE	COLLEGE OR UNIVERSITY
Alabama	Alabama A&M University
Alabama	Alabama State University
Alabama	Bishop State Community College
Alabama	Gadsden State Community College
Alabama	J.F. Drake State Community and Technical College
Alabama	Lawson State Community College
Alabama	Miles College
Alabama	Oakwood University
Alabama	Selma University
Alabama	Shelton State Community College
Alabama	Stillman College
Alabama	Talladega College
Alabama	Trenholm State Community College
Alabama	Tuskegee University
Arkansas	University of Arkansas at Pine Bluff
Arkansas	Arkansas Baptist College
Arkansas	Philander Smith College
Arkansas	Shorter College
Delaware	Delaware State University
District of Columbia	University of the District of Columbia
District of Columbia	Howard University

State	College or University
Florida	Bethune–Cookman University
Florida	Edward Waters College
Florida	Florida Agricultural and Mechanical University
Florida	Florida Memorial University
Georgia	Albany State University
Georgia	Clark Atlanta University
Georgia	Fort Valley State University
Georgia	Interdenominational Theological Center
Georgia	Morehouse College
Georgia	Morehouse School of Medicine
Georgia	Morris Brown College (unaccredited until at least October 2020; up for candidacy)
Georgia	Paine College
Georgia	Savannah State University
Georgia	Spelman College
Kentucky	Kentucky State University
Kentucky	Simmons College of Kentucky
Louisiana	Dillard University
Louisiana	Grambling State University
Louisiana	Southern University at New Orleans
Louisiana	Southern University at Shreveport
Louisiana	Southern University and Agricultural and Mechanical College

STATE	COLLEGE OR UNIVERSITY
Louisiana	Xavier University of Louisiana
Maryland	Bowie State University
Maryland	Coppin State University
Maryland	University of Maryland Eastern Shore
Maryland	Morgan State University
Mississippi	Alcorn State University
Mississippi	Coahoma Community College
Mississippi	Hinds Community College
Mississippi	Jackson State University
Mississippi	Mississippi Valley State University
Mississippi	Rust College
Mississippi	Tougaloo College
Missouri	Harris–Stowe State University
Missouri	Lincoln University of Missouri
North Carolina	Barber–Scotia College
North Carolina	Bennett College
North Carolina	Elizabeth City State University
North Carolina	Fayetteville State University
North Carolina	Johnson C. Smith University
North Carolina	Livingstone College
North Carolina	North Carolina Agricultural and Technical State University

STATE	COLLEGE OR UNIVERSITY
North Carolina	North Carolina Central University
North Carolina	Shaw University
North Carolina	St. Augustine's University
North Carolina	Winston-Salem State University
Ohio	Central State University
Ohio	Payne Theological Seminary
Ohio	Wilberforce University
Oklahoma	Langston University
Pennsylvania	Cheyney University of Pennsylvania
Pennsylvania	Lincoln University
South Carolina	Allen University
South Carolina	Benedict College
South Carolina	Claflin University
South Carolina	Clinton College
South Carolina	Denmark Technical College
South Carolina	Morris College
South Carolina	South Carolina State University
South Carolina	Voorhees College
Tennessee	American Baptist College
Tennessee	Fisk University
Tennessee	Knoxville College

STATE	COLLEGE OR UNIVERSITY
Tennessee	Lane College
Tennessee	LeMoyne–Owen College
Tennessee	Meharry Medical College
Tennessee	Tennessee State University
Texas	Huston–Tillotson University
Texas	Jarvis Christian College
Texas	Paul Quinn College
Texas	Prairie View A&M University
Texas	Southwestern Christian College
Texas	St. Philip's College
Texas	Texas College
Texas	Texas Southern University
Texas	Wiley College
U.S. Virgin Islands	University of the Virgin Islands
Virginia	Hampton University
Virginia	Norfolk State University
Virginia	Virginia State University
Virginia	Virginia Union University
Virginia	Virginia University of Lynchburg
West Virginia	Bluefield State College
West Virginia	West Virginia State University

Online Institutions

These colleges or universities offer most or all of their degrees through digital platforms. Make sure to check if these are regionally or nationally accredited; this might be important if you plan on transferring to another university. They should be accredited by the Distance Education Accrediting Commission (DEAC), which is recognized and authorized by the United States Department of Education. I've tried marking them accordingly, but accreditations can change. Check their websites for the most updated accreditation information in the institution's "About" page.

STATE	COLLEGE OR UNIVERSITY	ACCREDITATION
Alabama	Columbia Southern University	Nationally
Arizona	Brighton College	Nationally
Arizona	Dunlap-Stone University	Nationally
Arizona	Harrison Middleton University	Nationally
Arizona	National Paralegal College	Nationally
Arizona	Penn Foster College	Nationally
California	Abraham Lincoln University	Nationally
California	Anaheim University	Nationally
California	California Coast University	Nationally
California	California Intercontinental University	Nationally
California	California Southern University	Regionally
California	Henley-Putnam School of Strategic Security, National American University	Regionally
California	University of the People	Nationally
California	Westcliff University	Regionally
Colorado	American Sentinel University	Regionally

STATE	COLLEGE OR UNIVERSITY	ACCREDITATION
Colorado	Aspen University	Nationally
Colorado	Holmes Institute, School of Consciousness Studies	Nationally
Colorado	McKinley College	Nationally
Colorado	U.S. Career Institute	Nationally
Colorado	William Howard Taft University	Nationally
District of Columbia	Quantic School of Business and Technology	Nationally
Georgia	American InterContinental University	Regionally
Georgia	Ashworth College	Nationally
Kansas	Grantham University	Nationally
Louisiana	NationsUniversity	Nationally
Montana	Apollos University	Nationally
Missouri	American Business and Technology University	Nationally
Missouri	City Vision University	Nationally
New Jersey	National Tax Training School	Nationally
New Mexico	EC-Council University	Nationally
New York	New York Institute of Photography	Nationally
Ohio	Lakewood College	Nationally
Oregon	American College of Healthcare Sciences	Nationally
Pennsylvania	Blackstone Career Institute	Regionally
Utah	New Charter University	Nationally

STATE	COLLEGE OR UNIVERSITY	ACCREDITATION
Virginia	American National University	Nationally
Virginia	Atlantic University	Nationally
Virginia	University of Management and Technology	Nationally
West Virginia	Catholic Distance University	Nationally

Veteran-Serving Institutions

If you are a veteran student or family member of veterans, you might have specific concerns about how a school can support your studies. For example, does the school offer solid mental health counseling? Can they accommodate veterans with disabilities? Are any of the counselors or staff veterans themselves? Are there campus and social networking events planned especially for veterans? Can career center staff help veteran students identify job opportunities specifically geared toward them? Does the university have industry-employer relationship programs for both active duty and veteran students to help raise chances of post-graduation employment?

VIQTORY, a service-disabled, veteran-owned small business, labels schools Military Friendly® if they have a high rate of student retention, graduation, job placement, and loan repayment for veteran students. Below are some of the public colleges and universities that received their "Top Ten" friendliest ranking.

STATE	COLLEGE OR UNIVERSITY
Colorado	Colorado State University, Pueblo
Colorado	Front Range Community College
Colorado	University of Colorado, Boulder
Colorado	University of Colorado, Colorado Springs
Connecticut	Central Connecticut State University
Connecticut	Quinebaug Valley Community College
Delaware	University of Delaware
Florida	Florida Atlantic University

STATE	COLLEGE OR UNIVERSITY
Florida	Palm Beach State College
Florida	University of Florida
Florida	University of West Florida
Georgia	Central Georgia Technical College
Georgia	Chattahoochee Technical College
Georgia	Georgia State University
Georgia	Gwinnett Technical College
Georgia	Savannah Technical College
Georgia	University of Georgia
Georgia	West Georgia Technical College
Indiana	Vincennes University
Kansas	The University of Kansas
Michigan	Delta College
Michigan	Eastern Michigan University
Michigan	Northern Michigan University
Minnesota	Minnesota West Community and Technical College
Minnesota	Southwest Minnesota State University
Mississippi	Mississippi Gulf Coast Community College
Mississippi	Mississippi State University
Mississippi	The University of Southern Mississippi
Ohio	Clark State Community College

STATE	COLLEGE OR UNIVERSITY
Ohio	Cuyahoga Community College
Ohio	Kent State University, Columbiana County
Ohio	Ohio University
Oklahoma	Oklahoma State University, Oklahoma City
Maryland	Wor-Wic Community College
New Jersey	Kean University
New Mexico	The University of New Mexico
New York	The City University of New York, College of Staten Island
New York	The City University of New York, York College
New York	State University of New York, Maritime College
New York	State University of New York, Ulster County Community College
North Carolina	Cape Fear Community College
North Carolina	Elizabeth City State University
North Carolina	Fayetteville Technical Community College
North Carolina	North Carolina State University
North Dakota	University of North Dakota
Pennsylvania	University of Pittsburgh
South Dakota	South Dakota School of Mines & Technology
Texas	Angelo State University
Texas	Texas State Technical College
Texas	Texas State University

STATE	COLLEGE OR UNIVERSITY
Texas	The University of Texas at San Antonio
Virginia	Northern Virginia Community College
Virginia	Piedmont Virginia Community College
Virginia	Southwest Virginia Community College
Wisconsin	University of Wisconsin, Whitewater

Women's Colleges and Universities

These colleges or universities admit only female students. Some women's colleges have started creating policies that are inclusive of transgender students. Many are religiously affiliated, liberal arts schools.

STATE	COLLEGE OR UNIVERSITY
Alabama	Judson College
California	Mills College
California	Mount Saint Mary's University
California	Scripps College
District of Columbia	Trinity Washington University
Georgia	Agnes Scott College
Georgia	Spelman College
Georgia	Wesleyan College
Indiana	Saint Mary's College
Maryland	Notre Dame of Maryland University, Undergraduate Women's College
Massachusetts	Bay Path University

State	College or University
Massachusetts	Mount Holyoke College
Massachusetts	Simmons University, Undergraduate Program
Massachusetts	Smith College, Undergraduate Program
Massachusetts	Wellesley College
Minnesota	College of Saint Benedict
Minnesota	St. Catherine University
Missouri	Cottey College
Missouri	Stephens College
Nebraska	College of Saint Mary
New Jersey	Assumption College for Sisters
New York	Barnard College
New York	Russell Sage College
New York	Stern College for Women, Yeshiva University
North Carolina	Bennett College
North Carolina	Meredith College
North Carolina	Salem College
Ohio	Ursuline College
Pennsylvania	Bryn Mawr College
Pennsylvania	Cedar Crest College
Pennsylvania	Moore College of Art & Design
Virginia	Hollins University

STATE	COLLEGE OR UNIVERSITY
Virginia	Mary Baldwin College for Women, Mary Baldwin University
Virginia	Sweet Briar College
Virginia	Westhampton College, University of Richmond
Wisconsin	Alverno College (some co-ed undergraduate majors)
Wisconsin	Mount Mary University, Undergraduate Program

7. COLLEGE RANKINGS

Popular publications such as *U.S. News & World Report*, *Forbes*, and *The Wall Street Journal* publish rankings of United States colleges and universities each year. However, there are many ways to rank an institution; there is no clear "champion" university.

For example, taking the most recent 2020 rankings from the U.S. News & World Report, here are the "top" colleges and universities, sorted by different criteria.

CRITERIA	#1	#2	#3
National University	Princeton Univ.	Harvard Univ.	Columbia Univ.
Public Schools	Univ. of California, Los Angeles	Univ. of California, Berkeley	Univ. of Michigan, Ann Arbor
Best Value Schools	Princeton Univ.	Harvard Univ.	Yale Univ.
Most Innovative	Arizona State Univ. Tempe	Georgia State University	Massachusetts Institute of Technology
Social Mobility	Univ. of California, Riverside	Univ. of California, Santa Cruz	Univ. of California, Irvine
Undergraduate Teaching	Princeton Univ.	Elon Univ.	Brown Univ.
Colleges for Veterans	Stanford Univ.	Dartmouth College	Cornell Univ.

Other popular ranking criteria include:

- Best Four-Year Graduation Rates
- Best Business Programs
- Best Commuting Campuses
- Best Economic Diversity
- Best Engineering Programs
- Best Ethnic Diversity on Campus
- Best First-Year Experiences
- Best Fraternities
- Best Freshman Retention Rate
- Best Housing on Campus
- Best International Student Support Programs

- Best Internship Programs
- Best Learning Communities
- Best Liberal Arts Colleges
- Best Private Universities
- Best Public Universities
- Best Outcomes for Graduates
- Best Regional School
- Best Scholarship Programs
- Best School by Size (small/medium/large)
- Best Senior Capstone Projects
- Best Service Learning Programs
- Best Sororities
- Best Student Engagement
- Best Study Abroad Programs
- Best Transfer Programs
- Best Undergraduate Research/Creative Projects
- Best Value Schools
- Best Writing Programs

When considering which institution you would like to attend, go beyond the simple "national university" standard. Of course, having a degree from Princeton, Harvard, or Columbia would do you well because of the universities' fame and exclusivity. However, is that really the right school for *you*? Columbia University, for example, is right in the middle of Manhattan. Is that where you want to live for four years? Unless you qualify for a full scholarship, this school and the other national leaders cost a lot of money. Are you comfortable with graduating with loans? Perhaps you answer "yes" to both of these. In that case, you should definitely apply. However, if you answer "no," it might be good for you to consider other ways to evaluate institutions. Perhaps social justice matters a lot to you. Some institutions are much more engaged in ethical practices and social justice than others are. Perhaps class size and the quality and quantity of professor-student interactions is a key deciding factor for you. If so, then a large university might not be the right fit. In any case, you should spend as much time as possible researching institutions and evaluating them on the criteria that matter to *you*.

8. CAMPUS VISITS

When I applied to Columbia University for graduate school, I had never been east of Nevada. I was thinking about moving to New York City, but I had never even seen falling snow before. I had been to Tokyo already, which is one of the biggest cities in the world, so I wasn't afraid of crowds. But not all big cities are the same. And some would say that there is no other city like New York! All I could do was try to visit the city for a few days, visit the campus, and make this huge decision based off that short experience.

I booked a flight that would land in New York on a Thursday and leave on Sunday. It would give me a day and a half to see the campus, then another day and a half to see the city. The date was June 25, 2009. I can remember the date easily now because it was an important day in American cultural history: the day Michael Jackson died. I took the train from the airport to Times Square. The news of his death was flashing across all of the electronic ticker boards around the square. I watched people publicly react with shock and extreme sadness, crying on the street. I also saw New Yorkers do something very particular: they comforted each other, complete strangers. People started chatting with each other about their favorite Michael Jackson songs, about his scandals and his trial, about how our society probably killed him. Back home in California, people are friendly and engage in small talk, but this kind of comforting each other was new to me. It was my first glimpse of New York culture.

I found a hostel just a few blocks away from the campus. The hostel was very cheap if I stayed in a room with twelve beds. In my room were people from all over the world who came to see the city. My bunkmate was from Switzerland. Across from us were two guys from Italy. We all decided to go see Brooklyn together on Saturday. Before that, however, I needed to spend time around the campus in Morningside Heights and figure out if Columbia was the place for me.

The first thing I noticed was all of the delis and small shops. I was from a suburban city near Los Angeles; big shopping malls and major brand-name supermarkets were the most common near me. Here in New York City, there were countless places to buy things yet not many one-stop shopping places. Would I like shopping like this every day or not? The next thing I noticed was the fashion on campus: luxury brands. We have an outlet mall in the city where I'm from, but the luxury brands I saw on campus are not sold at outlet shops. I went to public schools my whole life, and I was not a rich kid by any means. Would I be able to fit in with students from these economic and social backgrounds?

I found a welcome center, and I scheduled a campus tour for later that day. Three current Columbia students from different majors led the tour. As we walked across the beautiful campus and in and out of the old and new buildings, they told us all of the interesting facts about the school and its history. World leaders often teach courses on campus. The French language department building used to be an insane asylum. *Ghostbusters* (1984) was filmed on campus, and the profits from the franchise help finance all of the university landscaping. The Columbia University Libraries is a system of twenty-two libraries. Twenty-two?! When they brought us inside Butler Library, I was sold. I had never seen so many books, never been in such a gorgeous study space, and never heard of such scholarly resources before. Seeing the city and getting a feel for the neighborhood were important parts of my visit, but the campus tour was the most important. It convinced me that I was willing to make a big step and move to New York to attend Columbia. The delicious Jamaican beef patties I had in Brooklyn with my hostel roommates on Saturday didn't make my decision any harder either.

If possible, visit the schools to which you are accepted. If you are entering graduate school in a funded program, your prospective department might even pay for your flight and accommodations so that you can visit the school. For some students, there are important questions that you will want answers to, and the school website might not answer all of them. You could ask the campus tour guides the questions. Even better, you could ask random students you meet on campus.

Try to find a public place where students look like they are relaxing, such as the common outside space with benches and an open field or the cafeteria. Don't bother students who are studying in the library or rushing to a class. Once you find a small group of students to talk to (a small group is better than just one student because you'll get multiple answers at once), ask a few questions. Here are a few of my favorite from the Princeton Review's website:

The Basics
- Why did you choose this school?
- Are you happy here?
- What's your biggest complaint about this school?

Academics
- What's your favorite class you've taken?
- Are your professors easy to meet in office hours?
- Are most of your classes taught by professors or by teaching assistants?
- Do students here use the writing center?
- Is the academic advising center helpful?

Campus Life
- What do you do when you're not in class?
- How's the food on campus? How about off campus?
- How are the dorms?
- Which clubs and student organizations are popular?
- What's your favorite place to study on campus?
- Are there enough computer labs?
- How is the Wi-Fi on campus?

Student Body
- How would you describe your fellow students?
- Are the students here friendly?
- Is there diversity on campus?

Career Services

- Is the career center helpful?
- Do employers recruit on campus?
- Is it easy to find summer jobs on or around campus?

Just because you crossed the bridge once doesn't mean you can't turn around and go home. Before you decide to move permanently, take a short trip over the bridge and see what life is like on the other side. Just make sure you don't burn the bridge down on your way over—do you have enough money to return? Do you have a place to which you can return?

Self-Reflection/Discussion Questions:

1. Have you ever visited a college campus? What was your first experience like?
2. Are there certain locations or environments, such as rural, suburban, or metropolitan, that you would not want to study in? Why?
3. Would you be intimidated to ask random students on campus questions during

9. COLLEGE WEBSITES AND OTHER INTERNET RESOURCES

College websites can be very confusing and intimidating to navigate. Some use industry-leading web platforms and are very dynamic while others look like they haven't been updated in years. Some make finding the information you're looking for very simple while others almost seem to be hiding things from you on purpose. Unless you live near the college you want to attend, you will often have to rely on its website for most of your initial information. Therefore, it is worth getting to know its website and how to navigate it.

Check out a few of the homepages for these colleges and universities below, some of which I have attended or worked at. Try them both on a desktop and on your mobile device. What similarities do you notice in their interfaces? What differences? Which is the easiest to navigate? Which is the hardest? Which do you prefer?

- Brigham Young University (large, private Mormon university)
- California State Polytechnic University, Pomona (large, public polytechnic university)
- Colorado School of Mines (small, public technological university)
- Columbia University (large, private university)
- College of the Holy Cross (small, private Jesuit Catholic university)
- Massachusetts Institute of Technology (medium, private institute of technology)
- Metropolitan Community College (large, public two-year college)
- New York University Shanghai (small, international campus of large, private university)
- University of Portland (small, private university)
- Temple University, Japan Campus (small, international campus of large, public university)
- The University of Texas at Austin (large, public university)

The below information on navigating college websites and this section's Self-Reflection/Discussion Questions are remixed from the open textbook A Different Road to College, pp. 72-74:

Colleges will often cater the organization of their website for different types of students. These types might include:

- **New:** You've never attended any college.
- **Returning:** You were previously enrolled at this college, you took time off, and now you're coming back.
- **Transferring:** You were a student at another college, and now you're coming to this one.
- **Students requiring accommodations:** You have a temporary or permanent disability that requires special accommodations, especially during the admissions process.
- **Local residents:** You are an "in-state" student who lives around the campus.
- **Veterans:** You are either on active duty or are inactive and will attend classes.
- **International:** You are a resident of a foreign country and will be attending this university on a student visa.

- **Credit:** You will take classes that bear credit, moving you toward the completion of a certificate or degree.
- **Non-credit or community education:** You will take classes that do not bear credit, and you are not seeking to complete a certificate or degree.
- **Continuing or adult education:** You are taking classes in the evening and/or on weekends that may or may not lead to completing a certificate or degree.

Whether you agree with this organization or not, you probably fit into one of these categories more than you do another. You will need to figure out which one is yours. Luckily, many schools' front webpage will have a button that reads something like "Getting Started." If you can find this type of button, then you might have a better chance of figuring out which category pertains to you. Another tool is the search bar. If you can find a search bar on the front page, try typing in a few of these keywords to learn about important aspects of the college: "mission statement," "strategic plan," "vision," "enrollment," "location," "application," "deadline," "residency," "student conduct code," "student rights and responsibilities," "placement test," "test scores," "financial aid," or "success stories."

Beyond individual college websites, there are large websites that gather lots of information about colleges all over the country. Some useful websites to check out include:

College Affordability and Transparency Center, which is a portal website run by the United States Department of Education to meet requirements in the Higher Education Opportunity Act. From this portal, you can access:

- College Affordability and Transparency List, which is a report generator that answers questions such as "Which colleges have the highest and lowest tuition and net prices?" or "How much do career and vocational programs cost?" or "How fast are college costs going up?" You can also download archived data files dating back to 2011.
- College Navigator, which is a tool created by the National Center for Education Statistics for finding both general and very specific information about colleges and universities across the United States. General information includes the university website address, type of university, degrees offered, campus setting, availability of campus housing, student population, and student-to-faculty ratio. Specific information includes tuition and estimated student expenses, financial aid availability, enrollment figures, admissions requirements, retention and graduation rates, outcome measures, programs and majors, services for veterans, varsity athletic teams, accreditation information, campus security information, and student loan default rates. You can search for schools by name, state, zip code, level of degree/award, and institution type.
- College Scorecard, which is a tool for comparing colleges and universities. You can compare by programs and degrees, location, size, type of school, and religious affiliation. After you have chosen what schools to compare, you can sort institutions based on average annual cost, graduation rate, or salary after attending.

College Board, which runs the AP® exams and the SAT® test. From this website, you can access:

- Big Future, which offers free college planning information and help with searching for schools, choosing majors, applying for scholarships, and planning for a career.

Strive for College, which is a system of free college and career matching services, including:

- UStrive, which is a free college mentoring service for help with college applications, financial aid documents, career opportunities, and more.
- I'm First, which is an online community celebrating and supporting first-generation college students.

Visiting every campus physically would be tiresome and costly. Luckily, the internet is a digital bridge that connects people and places from all around the world. Make sure you know how to use it. It's one of the best resources you have in preparing to physically cross that bridge later.

Self-Reflection/Discussion Questions:

1. Have you ever visited a university's website? If so, how comfortable were you navigating the site?
2. What information on a college website is most important to you as a student?
3. Do you think it's important that your university is good at using social media? What kinds of social media platforms should universities be taking most advantage of?
4. As a student, how can you use the college website, social media, and the internet in general to strengthen your own learning community?

10. APPLICATIONS

Did you know?

* Most colleges and universities will answer questions about their applications and even walk you through filling out their application at their welcome center or at their admissions office. Don't be afraid to go to the school and get help! Filling out the application is the most important step to getting in. Without a complete and correct application, you can't get in! Therefore, do it with enough time and do it right!

First, be aware that some schools will have their own unique applications that you must fill out. These could be on paper, but most schools have moved to digital submissions. For digital submissions, you will need to create an account on the school's application website. Sometimes, you will need to wait twenty-four to forty-eight business hours for a "welcome email" before you can access the application. Therefore, if the deadline is on a Friday at 17:00, make sure you create an account well before Wednesday. If you create that account late on Thursday, you might not even get access to the application until Monday. For schools that require these unique applications, there might be specific questions that other schools never ask you as well as special document requirements.

Next, know that many schools might use a shared application program through which you can apply to many schools. Common App is a non-profit service used by almost 900 United States colleges and universities, both domestically and with international campuses in Australia, Bulgaria, Canada, China, Czech Republic, France, Germany, Hong Kong, Ireland, Italy, Japan, Latvia, Lebanon, Qatar, Singapore, South Korea, Spain, Switzerland, and the United Kingdom. You fill out one online application, and you can use that application to apply to any of these participating schools around the world. In 2019, Common App teamed up with former First Lady Michelle Obama's Reach Higher college access initiative in order to promote applying to college as something easy, fun, and important to do.

If you go to the Common App website, you can create a free "practice account" by choosing the "Parent or other adult" option. This is especially worth doing if you will apply to many schools that use the Common App. Try filling out the practice application without any risk of accidentally submitting a bad application. You can even convert your practice account into a real account once you're ready to submit, meaning that you won't have to retype all of your information into the system again. Simply e-mail The Common Application's Solution Center (appsupport@commonapp.net) with your full name, date of birth, and a statemen that you want to change your practice account into an applicant account. Applying to college takes a lot of time, so find any ways like this that save you time and effort.

There are two types of applications I will discuss below: undergraduate and graduate school.

Undergraduate School

Typically, a complete undergraduate application will include the application form itself plus the submission of proof of completing high school or its equivalent. International students will also have to submit documents such as a copy of their passport, a proof of funding form, a proof of English language proficiency form, certified English translations of their high school diploma documents, a copy of their F-1 visa form and all prior I-20 forms, and others. You will need to ask your school's visa coordinator or center for international students for specific answers.

At some schools, international students don't need to prove their English language skills if they:

- Come from countries where English is a first or official language.
- Have a diploma from a United States high school.
- Graduated with an International Baccalaureate (IB).
- Received a C grade or higher from a college level English class at an accredited college or university in the United States.

However, you should ask the academic advising staff at your school about its specific requirements.

College and university applications evaluate you on many different things. Here are some of the most basic yet important things to focus on for your application:

- Submit it before the deadline. This is the first and most essential aspect evaluated of you as a student: time management and responsibility. Submit a complete application before the deadline.
- Submit it correctly and completely. This is another important aspect of being a good college student: reading carefully, preparing everything you need, and submitting what is asked of you.
- Submit it without errors. Good college students should also be detail-oriented and careful. Proofread your application. This doesn't mean "use spell-check." I mean read every word aloud to yourself. Spell-check will catch simple errors, but if you use correct English words in the wrong place, it won't catch them. Read it aloud.
- Submit enough. If essay response sections have word counts or character counts, stick to them. Show the admissions staff that you can pay attention and meet requirements.
- Submit what they want. If essay response sections have specific prompts, answer the questions they ask or write on the topic they request. Show the admissions staff, again, that you can pay attention and meet requirements. Here are some common essay questions, remixed from the open textbook *A Different Road to College*, pp. 113:

  o Explain your career aspirations and your educational plan to meet these goals. Be specific.
  o Explain how you've helped your family or made your community a better place to live. Provide specific examples.
  o Describe a personal accomplishment and the strengths and skills you used to achieve it.
  o Describe a significant change or experience that has occurred in your life. How did you respond and what did you learn about yourself?

Your answers to any of these questions do not need to be "world-saving." Instead, just try to show your personality and best qualities. Tell small, specific stories to maximize the word count limit you're given.

- Familiarize yourself with the school. If the application asks you why you want to attend that school, then show that you know something about it. What majors are popular at the school? What programs are particularly strong? What about the campus community attracts you?
    - If it's possible, visit the campus before you apply. Speak with the welcome center staff, and ask them to direct you to key places on campus where you can learn about the school's history and culture. Talk to as many students and staff on site as possible. You can use these stories later in a narrative for your application essay.
    - If you can't visit the campus, immerse yourself in the institution's website and social media accounts. Learn as much as you can about how the school views itself and how it is viewed from the outside (in newspapers, on blogs, or in videos).
    - Find out if you know any alumni members. Maybe someone in your family went to the school. Maybe one of your family member's friends went. Look up your local governmental representative (city councilperson or mayor) and see if they went to that school. If so, see if you can meet and speak with any of these people to learn about their experiences.

Graduate School

Typically, a graduate school application will include the application itself plus the submission of proof of completing an undergraduate degree. International students will also have to submit documents such as a copy of their passport, a proof of funding form, a proof of English language proficiency form, a copy of their F-1 visa form and all prior I-20 forms, and others. You will need to ask your school's visa coordinator or center for international students for specific answers.

At some schools, international students don't need to prove their English language skills if they:

- Come from countries where English is a first or official language.
- Have a diploma from a United States high school.
- Graduated with an International Baccalaureate (IB).
- Received a C grade or higher from a college level English class at an accredited college or university in the United States.

However, you should ask the academic advising staff at your school about their specific requirements.

Graduate school applications evaluate you on many different things. Here are some of the most basic yet important things to focus on for your application:

- Submit it before the deadline. This is the first and most essential aspect evaluated of you as a student: time management and responsibility. Submit a complete application before the deadline.
- If you have to submit letters of recommendation as part of your application, make sure that you request letters from your professors far in advance. I recommend asking at least three weeks in advance. Make sure that your professors know when the letters are due. Incomplete applications due to missing letters of recommendation can be rejected. Therefore, plan!
  - o Some institutions will allow faculty recommenders to send their letters in a simple email. Others will require that you request a letter from that faculty recommender using a secured web service. As soon as that school's application portal is open, figure out what is required and how to get those things submitted. Confusion about submitting these required items can be disastrous for your application.
- Submit it correctly and completely. This is another important aspect of being a good graduate student: reading carefully, preparing everything you need, and submitting what is asked of you.
  - o If you have to submit official transcripts as part of your application, request them from your school well in advance. They can sometimes take multiple days to be processed and sent. Some universities will ask that they arrive directly from your undergraduate institution. This request and delivery process can take more time than you think. Plan!
- Submit it without errors. Good graduate students should also be detail-oriented and careful. Proofread your application. This doesn't mean "use spell-check." Read every word aloud to yourself. Spell-check will catch simple errors, but if you use correct English words in the wrong place, it won't catch them. Read it aloud.
- Submit enough. If essay response sections have word counts or character counts, stick to them. Show the admissions staff that you can pay attention and meet requirements.
- In your statement of purpose essay, you should be specific about what area you would like to focus on, but not so specific that you sound like you only want to study one very particular thing. For example, it would be safe enough to say you wanted to study "twentieth century American literature" if you were applying for a doctoral program in English. If your statement only said you wanted to study "American literature," it would sound too broad, unfocused, and almost insincere about wanting to go to graduate school. If your statement said "twentieth century novellas written by Texan women about prohibition," it sounds like you definitely know what you want to do, but it might be so specific that you won't find many faculty members with which to study the subject.
- In your statement of purpose essay, you should mention which faculty members you want to work with in the program you're applying to and why. Show that you know

who teaches in the program, what courses they teach, and what research they have done in the field that interests you.

- o In the humanities, you do not need to contact a professor in advance to ask if they will take you as a graduate student. This is not a common agreement/situation at United States universities. In fact, this might bother some professors or make the evaluation process of your application uncomfortable. Instead, simply do your research on who is teaching graduate-level courses at that university, and mention that you'd like to study with them in your application. This is enough.

- o In the sciences, many prospective students do contact a professor in advance to ask if they can take on new graduate students. These professors might be running labs using grant money that only has a certain amount allocated to pay for graduate assistant stipends. Therefore, you should do your research on who is teaching graduate-level courses at that university, but you should also contact that professor with a statement of interest and a query about their availability. If that professor writes you back and explains they cannot take new graduate students, it will save you the time and disappointment of applying and being rejected.

Getting Through

Photo by Shawn Higgins

11. COMMON CHALLENGES

The first thing on my mind when I arrived at Columbia University as a master's student at the age of twenty-two was money. Not the money I imagined making because I was going to graduate from an Ivy League university; the money I needed to pay for school and for living in New York City's Manhattan. I applied for financial aid, which included a package of loans and the university's work-study program. A week after I arrived on campus, I received an email from the Department of Middle East and Asian Languages and Cultures (MEALAC, at the time, now known as MESAAS for Middle Eastern, South Asian, and African Studies). They received my information from the financial aid office and interviewed me for a research assistant position. They told me I would be working for a newly hired professor who was coming down from McGill University in Canada. This professor would be taking on something called an "endowed title" in the department, meaning he was highly respected even among Columbia's other outstanding professors. Honestly, I had never heard of McGill, even though it is one of Canada's most prestigious universities. And, admittedly, I had never heard of the professor for whom I was going to be working, even though he is one of the most famous in the field of Islamic law studies: Dr. Wael Hallaq.

The day Dr. Hallaq arrived on campus, I went to greet him in his office. My task for the day was to help him get set up on campus by unpacking his many boxes of books and arranging his bookshelves. I went to his office, and I found him standing inside. He had silver hair, strong black eyebrows, and a wonderfully warm smile. He came forward to shake my hand and introduce himself, but he had a look of concern on his face. He politely asked me: "Do you understand Arabic?" I earnestly looked at him and shook my head "no." He smirked and asked me a follow-up question: "Do you have any idea who I am?" Again, but this time with a nervous laugh, I honestly said "no." His smile grew, and as we shook hands, he concluded that our pairing as professor and research assistant would "be interesting."

In order to complete my first assignment of arranging his bookshelves, I needed to be familiar with Eastern Arabic numerals at minimum; most of his other research assistants in the past had been fluent in reading as well as speaking Arabic. I couldn't organize his periodicals and his multi-volume sets unless I knew which order they were supposed to go in, and Eastern Arabic (٠, ١, ٢, ٣, ٤, ٥, ٦, ٧, ٨ and ٩) is not the same as Western Arabic (the 0-9 system with which English users are familiar). To save myself from losing my job on the first day, I took out my newly acquired "smartphone" (they had just recently been invented) and pulled up a website on Eastern Arabic numerals. I showed it to the professor and assured him that I would learn as I organize. I found out weeks later that this move gave him all the confidence he needed in me; I was willing to learn, and that's the most important quality you can have as a research assistant. Our relationship grew as I helped him work on his book *The Impossible State: Islam, Politics, and Modernity's Moral Predicament* (Columbia UP, 2012), and he even thanked me as one of his "gifted and efficient research assistants" in the book's preface. It might have been much easier on that first day to excuse myself, say I wasn't the right person for the job, and ask the university for something better suited to my skills. However, I am so glad I challenged myself because I gained not only money and new skills but also a mentor along the way.

General Problem Solving

The general problem solving explanation and tips below are remixed from the open text-book College Success, pp. 64-65:

Even when you have clear goals, are motivated, and are focused, problems sometimes happen. First, you have to accept that they will happen; you can't avoid every problem. The difference between students who succeed by solving the problem and learning from it and those who get frustrated and give up is partly attitude and partly experience.

Many different kinds of setbacks may happen while you're in college (and in your life generally). Here are just a few examples:

- A financial crisis
- An illness or injury
- A crisis involving your family or loved ones
- Stress related to frequently feeling like you don't have enough time
- Stress related to relationship problems

Many other kinds of problems can be prevented or made less likely to occur. You can take steps to stay healthy. You can take control of your finances. You can learn how to build successful relationships to get along better with your instructors, classmates, and romantic partners. You can learn time management techniques to make sure you use your time effectively. However, some things happen that you cannot prevent, such as some illnesses or losing your job because of an economic recession or crises involving family members. Other problems, such as a social or relationship issue or an academic problem in a certain class, may be more complex and not easily prevented. What then?

First, work to resolve the immediate problem:

1. Stay motivated and focused. Don't let frustration or anxiety make the problem worse. Reassure yourself that the problem probably has a solution, and go into the problem-solving procedure confident and relaxed.
2. Analyze the problem and consider all possible solutions, not just the ones with which you are comfortable. For example, a financial problem doesn't automatically mean you have to drop out of school. You could take out student loans, cut back on living expenses, or take some time off school in order to save money and come back. You might not like any of these ideas, but they are possible solutions and can help you avoid dropping out entirely. Another example is failing a midterm exam. Failing a test doesn't always mean you will automatically fail the course. Instead, you can determine what went wrong, work with your instructor to improve your study plan, and use better strategies for the next exam. You might not like doing any of these things, but it's better than simply giving up.
3. Get help when you need it. None of us gets through life alone. It is not a sign of weakness to see your academic advisor, college counselor, the writing center staff,

or your professor when you have questions or problems. In fact, I think it is a clear sign of maturity and responsibility.

4. After you've developed a plan to resolve the problem, follow through. If solving the problem will take a while, track your progress in smaller steps so that you can see yourself actually succeeding.

After you've solved the problem, be sure to avoid it in the future:

1. You've crossed this bridge before. When you come to it again in the future, shouldn't you know the best way across?

2. Be honest with yourself. Were you the one who caused the problem? Did you contribute to it? Sometimes, the reasons are clear: you partied the night before the exam, you either became intoxicated or didn't sleep enough, and, as a result, you couldn't think clearly during the exam. Other times, you might not feel like it was your fault, but you contributed somehow. For example, if you are constantly catching colds or other illnesses that keep you from doing your best, consider your lifestyle. Do you wash your hands frequently enough? Are you dressed warmly enough in the winter? Are you sharing food and beverages with friends or exchanging germs in other ways? It's easy to say "It's not my fault; I was sick!," and, of course, that's true sometimes. But not always. If you don't honestly explore the factors that led to the problem, it's likely to happen again.

3. Take responsibility for your life and your role in what happens to you. Some people have negative attitudes and are always blaming others, fate, or "the system" for their problems. Of course, at times these outside forces do seem to be the biggest cause of our problems. However, unless you want to keep having problems, you need to figure out how to solve the issues that you're dealing with. No one will solve them for you.

4. Taking responsibility does not mean hating yourself. Failing at something does not make you a failure. We all fail at something, sometimes. And, honestly, I think the more you fail, the more you grow. Some people never fail at anything because they never take any risks with the option to fail. Fail and learn from it and grow. Adjust your attitude so that you're ready to try again. Feel happy knowing that you won't repeat mistakes you've made in the past.

5. Make a plan. Make effective use of your time. Change toxic behaviors. If you know that watching one YouTube video or one episode of a Netflix series can easily lead to you binge watching five more, avoid that initial toxic behavior. If you know that changing one part of your schedule will ultimately affect the rest of your daily schedule, do your best to stick to your regular schedule. Do whatever you can to make sure you use your time effectively and according to what you want to get done.

Money

One of the most common struggles college students face involves money. It can be difficult to find scholarships, pay tuition each semester, afford books and lab fees, find part-time jobs, and budget your finances through the semester. It is important that students know how to access financial aid.

Financial aid includes all the ways in which you get help with money to attend and pay for your university life. Financial aid might include help from your family, scholarships, grants, loans, or paid employment such as work-study programs. You can receive scholarships, loans, and work-study opportunities from your high school, a foundation, a corporation, or federal and state agencies such as the United States Department of Education. The most important difference in these terms is that scholarships and grants do not have to be paid back, while loans must be paid back. Some scholarships and grants are only available for people from specific countries, age ranges, races, ethnicities, religions, and so on. International students are typically not allowed to receive financial aid from the host country's government.

First, you should contact your school's financial aid office to learn about scholarships or grants available directly from your school. If you are awarded one of these, it is simply free money; you don't pay back scholarships or grants. After this, you could try the following to search for scholarships and grants:

- Fill out the FAFSA® (Free Application for Federal Student Aid) every year that you're in school. This application will help you qualify for grants such as the Pell Grant. This grant is free money that you will not need to pay back. Your school might also use your FAFSA to qualify you for a Federal Supplemental Educational Opportunity Grant (FSEOG), which is a grant you will not need to pay back.
- Consider your eligibility for aid benefits from the federal government through programs such as AmeriCorps, the Educational and Training Vouchers for Current and Former Foster Care Youth, the Indian Health Service's National Health Service Corps Loan Repayment Program, the National Institutes of Health's Division of Loan Repayment, or the National Health Service Corp's loan repayment program.
- If you have a parent or guardian who died in military service in Iraq or Afghanistan, you might qualify for an Iraq and Afghanistan Service Grant.
- If you plan to become a teacher in a high-need field in a low-income area, you might qualify for a TEACH Grant. While this grant is free money you do not need to pay back, it comes with a service obligation and other requirements. Please read into this carefully if you are interested in applying for it.
- Visit the CareerOneStop website, which is a searchable website of more than 8,000 scholarships, fellowships, and grants sponsored by the United States Department of Labor, Employment and Training Administration.
- Consider creating a free profile on Fastweb, where you can search and apply for over 1.5 million different college scholarships. This website is not maintained by the United States government.
- Beyond scholarships and grants, you still might find yourself struggling with finances during your college years. The below questions about and solutions to financial struggles are remixed from the open textbook College Success, pp. 410-419:

Taking control of your personal finances begins with thinking about your goals and deciding what matters to you. Here are some things to think about:

- Is it important to you that you graduate from college without debt? Is it acceptable to you, or necessary, or impossible, to take out some student loans?
- What are your priorities for summer sessions and other "free time"? Would you rather work to earn money or take a nonpaying internship or volunteering position to gain experience in your field? How will you incorporate social activities and time with friends and family into your college experience?
- How important is it to take a full load of classes so that your college education does not take longer than necessary or so that you meet visa requirements?
- How important is it for you to live in a nice place, drive a nice car, wear nice clothes, or eat in nice restaurants? How important are these things in comparison with your immediate educational goals?

Some students will realize that they have to work while they go to school in order to afford daily life. However, you have a choice in the types of jobs for which you apply. The best student jobs help you engage more deeply in the college experience, while the wrong kind of job gets in the way of that. Here are some factors to consider when you look for a job:

- What kinds of people will you be interacting with?
- Will you be working close to or far from campus?
- Is the job flexible enough to meet a college student's needs?
  - Can you change your work hours during final exam week or when a special project is due?
- What will you be able to say about your work on your future resume?

Another option for some students is to go into business for yourself. If you have energy, initiative, and some skill that is wanted by others, you can create your own work. For example, I built my own mobile DJ service while in college. I borrowed $500 from family members to purchase basic audio mixing equipment and speakers. I began DJing friends' parties at my college for free to advertise my skills. As my popularity grew, I was able to start charging for my services. I was able to pay back my family members and continue to earn money to buy improved equipment. This expansion allowed me to DJ larger, more prestigious parties that paid higher fees. Overall, my DJ business helped me pay for my entire undergraduate career when combined with the public university grants I received. Consider these other ways you can make money:

- Tutor classmates in a subject you are good in.
- Sell your technical skills to help others, such as setting up computer software, teaching people to use Microsoft Office, or designing websites.
- Sell things you no longer need. Earn commission by helping others sell things they don't need (this is especially good if you're skilled at social media services).

- Provide services to faculty members and residents in the nearby community, such as lawn mowing, snow shoveling, housecleaning, babysitting, pet sitting, dog walking, and more.
    - Professors, instructors, and graduate students who travel frequently for conferencing and research often need pet sitters and dog walkers. Reach out to them for these opportunities!

Even if you work, you still might find that you just don't have any money left at the end of the month. In this case, you might need to make adjustments in how you spend money on a daily basis. Remember, spending money does not define who you are. Follow some of these principles to spend less:

- Be aware of what you're spending. Carry a small notebook or download a free budget planning app to document everything you spend for a month. You'll see your habits, and you will see where you need to take control.
- Look for alternatives. Invest in a steel refillable bottle and seek out filtered drinking fountains instead of buying bottled water every day. Make coffee at home instead of going to a coffee shop every day. You can avoid many daily purchases by finding alternatives.
- Plan ahead to avoid impulse spending. Bring snacks in your bag to avoid buying things from expensive vending machines. Make a list before you go grocery shopping, and stick to only what's on the list. Only bring a certain amount of money out with you when you're eating and drinking with friends, and leave your credit card at home.
- Shop smart. Compare store prices, buy in bulk, and buy items when they are on sale.

Other tips for spending less include:

- Make your own lunches and snacks.
- Take advantage of your library's digital newspaper and magazine subscriptions instead of purchasing your own. Remember, you paid tuition, so you paid for access to these publications already. Don't pay twice!
- Cancel cable television and watch programs online for free. There is so much content available if you're willing to put up with advertisements!
- Cancel your private health club membership and exercise on campus if your school has a gym or at home doing body weight exercises and simple calisthenics.
- Look for free fun instead of going to movie theaters and concerts. Most colleges have free events happening throughout the year.
- If you pay your own utility bills, conserve energy. Make sure you turn off lights in your apartment and unplug electronics you're not currently using.
- Most importantly, don't fail classes! Paying to retake courses is one of the quickest ways to get in financial trouble.

Warning about Predatory Loans

When I was an undergraduate student (2003–2009), there was a fast-growing online loan company called MyRichUncle (which is now out of business). In the 2006 update to its website, MyRichUncle described itself as a "national student loan company offering federal and private loans to undergraduate, graduate, and professional students." MyRichUncle promised to "slash rates" on federal student loans such as the Stafford Loan, PLUS Loans, and Grad-PLUS loans. It also advertised its own unique system for making sure than any student with academic potential could qualify for loans.

In 2006, MyRichUncle took out an advertisement in *The New York Times* claiming that many colleges and universities had "pay-to-play" deals with money lending companies, meaning that the companies had to pay the schools to advertise their services to students as "preferred lenders." This led to attorney generals and others investigating the misconduct by universities. Investigators found corrupt lending practices happening at institutions such as Columbia University, Drexel University, Mercy College, Pace University, Seton Hall University, The University of Texas at Austin, Texas Tech, and Wayne State University. The result of this investigation was the creation of many state laws about student lending accountability and new regulations created by the Department of Education. However, as any quick internet search on "predatory student loans United States" will reveal, the problem is not yet fixed.

As the Legal Services Center of Harvard Law School (LSC) explains, student borrowers have the federal right to cancel their loans if their institutions are found to be corrupt and engaged in misconduct. However, the Department of Education is not necessarily trying to find these institutions and stop their deceitful practices. Instead of chasing after bad schools, the Department of Education seems more interested in forcing students to pay back these bad loans.

Visit the Federal Student Aid website and study it as carefully as possible. Here, you can find pages dedicated to types of financial aid, financial aid eligibility, FAFSA®, PLUS loans, promissory notes, loan repayments, loan forgiveness procedures and programs, and delinquency and defaulting. Do not sign up for loans without trying your best to understand all of their terms and conditions. The Federal Student Aid website has a "Glossary" page that briefly explains important key terms. Study and understand this, but, if you're able to do so, go beyond this page and speak with a financial consultant to understand more fully the importance and legal definitions of these terms. You have to pay back your loans, even if you later claim that you didn't understand what you were signing up for. Don't get trapped in a situation that you can't recover from. Please dedicate time and energy to understanding what loans will mean for you.

Getting Involved

Another common struggle most students face is getting fully engaged in their university lives. If you're a first-generation student, an international student, or a non-traditional student such as a commuter student (someone who lives off-campus), this struggle might feel particularly depressing. There are aspects of the university that are not welcoming to people like us in these categories. You will attend your classes and receive grades, but you might feel continuously left out or that you're not truly immersed in your college life. Particular struggles might include making friends, participating in on-campus activities, and interacting with faculty and staff. However, as hard as things might be, you have to find ways to overcome these struggles.

The possible solutions to these struggles in the bulleted list below are remixed from the open textbook No Limits, pp. 61:

- **Struggle:** Making friends on campus.
  - o **Solution:** Join a student organization.
  - o **Solution:** Invite classmates to join you for a study session or a snack break.
- **Struggle:** Making time to participate in on-campus activities.
  - o **Solution:** Start your day early. Arrive on campus early and get as much work done as possible in the morning hours. Then, you might have time for the social activities that often take place after classes finish.
  - o **Solution:** If you can't participate because you have an off-campus job, think about getting a job on campus. On-campus jobs will often be flexible with your hours if you explain that you want to attend a university function.
  - o **Solution:** Plan your schedule with big gaps in between classes. Try to make these gaps when events that you'd like to attend normally happen on campus. For example, if your department often hosts guest lectures at 15:00, make sure you're not taking class at the same time so that you can attend them. Don't put all of your classes back to back.
- **Struggle:** Interacting with staff and faculty.
  - o **Solution:** Meet with your professors in their office hours. Professors have very different personalities in front of the class and in their offices. If your professor seems intimidating in the classroom, you might find them to be much more friendly and approachable in a one-on-one setting.
  - o **Solution:** Join a student organization that has an active faculty advisor. This will give you a chance to get to know a professor outside of a graded classroom environment.
  - o **Solution:** Be on campus more. The more you see staff and faculty, the more normal they will become, and, therefore, less intimidating.

Time Management

An important thing you should know about being a student at a United States college or university is that you will be busy. To be successful, for each hour of class you take in a week, you should spend between two to three (or possibly more) additional hours outside of class working on things related to your studies. Being a "full-time student" is typically defined as taking at least twelve hours of classes per week. When you add this up, you can see that you will be spending between thirty-six and forty-eight hours both in and out of the class working on your academic studies. This amount of studying is a struggle for most students, especially those who want to do exceptionally well but have something in their lives that also requires many hours of their time such as a job, family obligations, a long commute, and so on.

The time management tips in the bulleted list below are remixed from the open textbook

No Limits, pp. 80:

- Use tools such as calendars (both physical and digital), to-do lists, sticky notes, planners, and learning management software (such as Blackboard and Canvas).
- Use the "wasted time" between classes to review notes, to read, to do homework, or to take care of personal affairs such as calling family members or doing any money-making business possible.
- Take short breaks instead of long ones. Work for thirty minutes and take a five minute break, or work for fifty minutes and take a ten minute break. Don't try to work for four hours straight with no break; you probably won't recover well after, and you'll actually get less work done.
- Figure out which activities require the most focus and energy, and plan to do those things when you feel most energized, especially if you dislike those activities. If you delay doing the difficult activities that you dislike, you might give up on doing them at the end of your day when your energy runs out.
- Study in a place and an environment without distractions. This includes impersonal forces (people you don't know, environmental noises) as well as personal forces (people you know, your cell phone). Figure out where you can study best; some people prefer the library, while others prefer their homes/rooms.
- Make sure you get enough sleep. Cut down on simple chatting with friends or mindless video watching, not sleep.

Dormmates/Roommates

Another new situation that many college students deal with is living on their own or away from their homes for the first time. Some universities require that all first-year students live on campus in dormitories. Some universities will allow students to live on campus for only one year while others might allow it for two, three, or even all four years. Some universities have many dorm options while others only have one or two. Some universities will have special dorms designated for married students, graduate students, and for students who are part of "living-learning communities" in which you live with people from your same major of study. If you live on campus, you will probably have dormmates or roommates if your dorm is particularly big. In these situations, you might struggle to get along with your co-residents. Struggles in your dorm can severely impact your ability to complete your studies.

The tips for getting along with your roommate in the bulleted list below are remixed from the open textbook No Limits, pp. 57:

- Try to get to know each other.
- Don't expect too much; you don't have to be best friends.
- Ask, listen, and discuss. Filling out a "roommate's agreement" early sets rules and boundaries for sharing personal items and space. For example, how late should friends be allowed over? How late should we allow the television to be on? How early is it okay to start making noise in the room?

- Be sensitive to each other's moods. Everyone has good and bad days, so try to be understanding.
- When things go wrong, discuss them. If you can't fix things between you, ask someone for help such as a resident assistant.

So Many Questions—Whom to Ask?

Another common challenge is simply not knowing whom to talk to on campus about the different kinds of questions you might have. There are so many bridges to cross, and you're just not sure which one will take you to the destination you have in mind. The list of college offices and resources below is remixed from the open textbook College Success, pp. 37-38:

- Academic advising office: This office helps you choose courses and plan your program or degree. You should have a meeting with them at least once every semester.
- Counseling office: This office helps with personal problems, including health, stress management, interpersonal issues, and so on.
- Financial aid office: This office deals with students currently receiving financial aid and can help you figure out if you qualify for financial assistance or not.
- Food pantry: Many colleges and universities provide free food to students in need. Students can't be successful if they don't eat, drink, and live well. Your college or university might offer food staples, household items, and personal care supplies either at a low cost or for free to students with current IDs. Schenectady County Community College, for example, offers dairy, grain, fruits, vegetables, protein, bath tissue, paper towels, laundry detergent, trash bags, deodorant, body wash, shampoo, toothpaste, shaving items, and other items to its students in need for free. Ask your college or university what supplies it offers its students in need. If it is not providing enough, consider forming a committee and creating a petition to ask the university to supply such items and services.
- Tutoring, writing, or skill centers: The title of this office changes depending on your specific college, but they are special places where students can go for additional help for their courses. A single center may help students with all academic skills, or your college may have separate centers for skills such as writing, math, and general studies.
- Computer labs: Many campuses have computer centers in which students can use both PC and Macintosh desktops as well as receive assistance with technical issues.
- Student health clinic: Your campus clinic will offer basic medical care and can make referrals to larger hospitals when needed. Most campus clinics can also help with issues such as diet and exercising concerns, birth control services, and preventative health care.
- Career center or placement office: This center offers a wide list of services for students and recent graduates. It can help you find an internship, find jobs to apply for, and learn more about specific companies. It can help you create and then review resumes and cover letters. It runs seminars on effective interviewing skills and on business etiquette. It often hosts company information sessions where a hiring manager or rep-

resentative from a company visits your campus to discuss future opportunities. Career services at your institution might also put on a "Career Fair," or a special day where students and recent graduates get to meet with many different employers in a central location such as your school's student union room or courtyard. If your institution does not host its own career fair, it can probably tell you where the closest career fair is happening, perhaps in a large city near you. Once you have an interview planned, career services can also help you prepare by offering you a mock interview session. At some schools, career services might even have a "Career Closet" filled with clothing you can borrow that will be suitable for your interview and a printing service to make up free business cards with your name on them.

- Office for students with disabilities: This office may provide various resources to help students with temporary or permanent disabilities adapt to the college environment.

- Housing office: This office not only controls campus housing but often assists students with finding off-campus private accommodations.

- Diversity office: This office promotes cultural awareness on campus, runs special programs, and assists students from diverse backgrounds with adjusting to campus culture.

- Office of student affairs or student services: This office can help you find ways to participate in campus activities and in organized groups. Organized groups on campus include student organizations, fraternities and sororities, clubs relating to diversity and inclusion, clubs relating to civic engagement and leadership, clubs relating to service and volunteerism, and student activity groups.

- Athletic center: Most colleges have exercise equipment, pools, courts and tracks, and other resources open to all students. If your college doesn't own its own facilities, then it might have deals with neighboring facilities so that students can use them. Athletic centers help students maintain their personal health, which then promotes academic success.

- Specialized offices for student populations: Your college might have individual offices for supporting students such as non-native English speakers, non-traditional students, international students, religious students, students with children (including a possible child care center), veteran students, students preparing for certain types of careers, and more.

- University ombuds: Oregon State University's website explains that this office can serve as a neutral or impartial facilitator for campus conflicts. This office does not have any official decision-making authority or disciplinary responsibilities. Students might visit the ombuds office for interpersonal/intercultural/group conflicts, confusion around policies or procedures on campus, ethical dilemmas, perceived unfair treatment or bullying, and any other concerns where you're not sure where to go to get a fair opinion.

- Campus police: Southeastern Oklahoma State University's website explains that campus police try to provide a safe university environment, protect life and property, investigate crimes and accidents, and give information and assistance when requested. Universities will often have police call boxes located across the campus in public places.

Campus police are often available twenty-four hours a day, seven days a week to help the campus community. Some schools have an escort service where students can request a ride home from a campus building late at night for extra safety.

Goal Setting

Finally, just know that getting through a United States college or university involves daily and long-term struggles to succeed. Some bridges are longer than others and require some serious dedication if you want to get to the other side. You need to keep your motivation high, and you need to know how to achieve your goals. Canadian entrepreneur and Olympic gold medalist in men's rowing Adam Kreek is quoted as having thought of goal creation in CLEAR terms. CLEAR goals are:

- Collaborative
- Limited
- Emotional
- Appreciable
- Refinable

You can apply this business model of goal achievement to your student life as well:

- **Collaborative:** Find any chance you can to work with others. Don't try to do college by yourself. Create a small, elite group of excellent students, and challenge and inspire each other to be better. I never would have made it through my community college, my undergraduate degree, or graduate school without collaboration.
- **Limited:** Everyone needs a break sometimes. And every project needs to finish at some point. Make sure your goals have a clear ending point, both in terms of the amount of work you do and the time that work takes you.
- **Emotional:** You have to care about what you're doing. Always connect your goals with a real emotion that affects you. Why are you in college? Why are you majoring in this field? What upsets you in the world that you want to change? What makes you sad? What makes you happy? What are your values?
- **Appreciable:** Break your large goal down into smaller goals. "Graduate from college" is a great goal, but smaller goals that will help you get there might include "Get at least an A- in all of my classes" or, even smaller, "Get at least an A- on the midterm exam." Achieving these smaller goals will get you one step closer to your ultimate goal.
- **Refinable:** Things happen, and sometimes we need to make changes to our plans. People get sick. People get hurt. People lose things. Sometimes, we just have some "bad luck" that we didn't expect. When these things happen to you, make sure you can look at that goal and adjust it to fit your new reality. This doesn't mean you just give up on that goal. Instead, you have to make sure that your goal has enough flexibility to be refined and modified to fit new circumstances. "Graduate from college" might have meant four years when you first wrote it down, but due to unforeseen circumstances, that might have to change to "Graduate from college in five years." Don't let setbacks

12. ACADEMIC ADVISING

"A joyful moment for me as an academic advisor is when I can help an advisee notice that they already have a good answer to the problem. Primarily, an advisor is expected to assist students by clarifying major/minor requirements and relevant school policies. This information is already available in the university bulletin and on the official website. However, many students seek guidance from an advisor because it is not always easy to make a good decision. For instance, a student couldn't make up her mind whether to choose the international business studies major for career success or to take the art major for her personal passion. It seemed to me that 'picking the best one' was her only thought. Instead, I suggested that she choose business as her major but also choose art as a minor. This idea excited her, and she thanked me for my 'simple solution.' For me, advising is a sort of Socratic education in which the advisor brings out a student's own ideas through questions and discussion."

—Shota Fujii
Academic Advisor, Temple University, Japan Campus

There is nothing more important for transferring to a university or graduating in a timely manner than planning your course schedule carefully. If you forget to take certain classes or take classes in the wrong order, it can cause major delays toward graduation. If you don't finish your general education classes before you start exploring a major, you might not be cleared to take higher-level classes. Similarly, you might not be able to transfer from your city college to a four-year university unless you complete your general education courses first. Remember the maze from the introduction of this book? Course planning is one of the clearest examples of how students with legacy knowledge get through college quicker than those students without it do. Luckily, you don't have to figure out your course schedule on your own. You should visit with your school's academic advising center each semester so that you can have a clear path to graduation.

Academic advising can be very helpful if you are planning to transfer to another institution. There are many kinds of transfers:

- Two-year college to four-year public or private university
- Four-year public university in your state to another in your state
- Four-year public university in your state to another outside of your state
- Four-year public university to a private university
- Private university to a four-year public university
- Private university to another private university
- University outside the United States to one inside the country

When a student transfers from one school to another, there are many possible outcomes. Hopefully, the progress you made at your current institution will directly transfer to the next. Most of the time, this will be the case if you transfer from one large public university to another. However, if you transfer between public and private universities, classes and learning outcomes will not always match. Therefore, while you qualify to be a junior (third-year) student at one institution, you might end up being a sophomore (second-year) student at your new institution. This is because your new institution has some foundational yet unique courses that you could not have taken at your previous institution and that you must complete before you can be "junior-standing." Similarly, transferring from a foreign university to a United States university can have many imbalances that affect your standing. While you might be a junior at your home institution, you might be a sophomore or even a freshman at your new institution if the credits you try to transfer cannot be equated with anything on your new campus. The frustrating part of transferring is that many institutions will not publicly post course equivalencies. Instead, the decision on whether a course from your previous institution counts or not is simply up to the review of staff at your new institution. Therefore, speaking with academic advising at both your current and your expected new institution is extremely important.

The academic and career planning timeline in the bulleted list below is my remix of the open textbook No Limits, pp. 195-197:

If you're attending a two-year college, read the following list. If you're attending a four-year university, skip down to the next set of bullet points. The two plans are similar, but the students at two-year colleges who do not plan on transferring have to plan for graduation and careers at a faster pace. For students at a two-year college:

- During your first year of college . . .
  - Meet with an academic advisor to plan your schedule. Make sure you are set to satisfy your college's core requirements. Start exploring different major options. Make an appointment each semester with an academic advisor to discuss your progress toward graduation.
  - Research which services your college's career center offers.
  - Attend two academic or professional seminars hosted by two different departments. You might hear a talk that interests you and persuades you to think more seriously about taking on a particular major.
  - Visit the career center and start looking over job listings. Just get an idea of what they look like and what kinds of jobs are being advertised at your college.
  - Get information from the career center about internships available for second-year students. You're not applying yet, but you should know what kinds of opportunities are available through your school.
  - Participate in student organizations and clubs to develop your leadership skills.
  - Attend a job fair. Don't try to talk to the representatives yet; you're not ready to apply. Just get an understanding of the environment. Notice how other student candidates are dressed, how they are prepared, and how they act. Notice which companies are present (and which are not that you would like to apply to).
- During your second/last year of college . . .
  - Make an appointment each semester with an academic advisor to discuss your progress toward graduation.

o Attend two career seminars (such as resume preparation or interview skills).

o Register for an internship (if it is important for students in your major).

o Develop a complete and effective resume and cover letter. Then, make an appointment with your career center to have them reviewed.

o Try to get a leadership position on campus, either in a student governmental organization or in a social or volunteer club.

o Make friends with graduating students in your major. Try to keep in touch with them as they search for jobs.

o Become familiar with at least three career options in your major. You can do this in consultation with your career center or by conducting "informational interviews" with working professionals. Sometimes, your career center or even your professors can help you set up these meetings with these professionals.

o If you're considering transferring to a four-year university, begin researching which universities your college has connections with. Some colleges are "feeder schools" for universities, meaning that university accepts many students from that college on a somewhat guaranteed basis as long as students meet certain requirements. However, you don't have to transfer to one of these local schools. Instead, you should research universities all across the country if you're interested. Seek out universities that have strong records in your major of interest, are in areas in which you'd like to move, or that provide resources and opportunities that interest you. Many colleges have transfer services offices at which you can receive information, advice, and support.

o Apply for graduation. You must apply to graduate. Simply completing all of your required classes will not guarantee that you "graduate." By applying for graduation, you are signaling to the college administration your plan to stop taking classes and to receive your degree. Some students, even after completing the classes for an associate degree, will continue taking classes in pursuit of a second associate degree or a certificate. Therefore, if you don't apply for graduation, the college will not know your intent. Also, make sure that you apply for graduation by the scheduled application date. For example, if you want to graduate in May, the application deadline might be in April or even March. If you do not apply in time, you will have to wait until the next graduation to receive your degree, which could be in December of that year. This delay might affect your job searching or your plans to transfer to a four-year university.

o Register with your career center's job listing service so that you can be informed about currently available positions for students in your major.

o Check with the career center for information on companies that will be doing interviews on your campus.

o Attend a job fair. This time, you're actually trying to get an interview. Come prepared, come professional, and come as yourself. First impressions are very important, so pace yourself and only talk to a representative when you're calm, confident, and ready.

The following bulleted list is for students attending a four-year university:

- During your first year of college . . .
  - o Meet with an academic advisor to plan your schedule. Make sure you are set to satisfy your university's core requirements. Start exploring different major options.
  - o Research which services your university's career center offers.
  - o Attend two academic or professional seminars hosted by two different departments. You might hear a talk that interests you and persuades you to think more seriously about taking on a particular major.
  - o Visit the career center and start looking over job listings. Just get an idea of what they look like and what kinds of jobs are being advertised at your university.
  - o Start writing a resume. Take note of big projects, activities, and committee work you do, as well as any university honors you receive while you're a student.
  - o Participate in student organizations and clubs to develop your leadership skills.
  - o Attend a job fair. Don't try to talk to the representatives yet; you're not ready to apply. Just get an understanding of the environment. Notice how other student candidates are dressed, how they are prepared, and how they act. Notice which companies are present (and which are not that you would like to apply to).
- During your second year of college . . .
  - o Visit academic advising to talk about the grades you received in your first year. Get their opinion about what major you seem best fit for.
  - o Get information from the career center about internships available for third- and fourth-year students. You're not applying yet, but you should know what kinds of opportunities are available through your school.
  - o Start writing a resume. Take note of big projects, activities, and committee work you do, as well as any university honors you receive while you're a student.
  - o Attend two more academic seminars in fields very different than what you attended in your first year. You might have an idea of what you want to major in, but perhaps you've never thought of these other fields. Before you dedicate yourself to a particular major, make sure you've thought about every option.
  - o Once you have weighed your major options carefully, apply to and get accepted into a department for your major.
  - o Attend a job fair. Don't try to talk to the representatives yet; you're not ready to apply. Just get an understanding of the environment. Notice how other student candidates are dressed, how they are prepared, and how they act. Notice which companies are present (and which are not that you would like to apply to).
- During your third year of college . . .
  - o Make an appointment each semester with an academic advisor to discuss your progress toward graduation.
  - o Attend two career seminars (such as resume preparation or interview skills).
  - o Register for an internship (if it is important for students in your major).
  - o Develop a complete and effective resume and cover letter. Then, make an appointment with your career center to have them reviewed.

- o Try to get a leadership position on campus, either in a student governmental organization or in a social or volunteer club.
- o Make friends with graduating students in your major. Try to keep in touch with them as they search for jobs.
- o Become familiar with at least three career options in your major. You can do this in consultation with your career center or by conducting "informational interviews" with working professionals. Sometimes, your career center or even your professors can help you set up these meetings with these professionals.
- o Attend a job fair. Don't try to talk to the representatives yet; you're not ready to apply. Just get an understanding of the environment. Notice how other student candidates are dressed, how they are prepared, and how they act. Notice which companies are present (and which are not that you would like to apply to).
- • During your fourth year of college . . .
  - o Apply for graduation. You must apply to graduate. Simply completing all of your required classes will not guarantee that you "graduate." By applying for graduation, you are signaling to the university administration your plan to stop taking classes and to receive your degree. Some students, even after completing the classes for a bachelor's degree, will continue taking classes in pursuit of a second major. Therefore, if you don't apply for graduation, the university will not know your intent. Also, make sure that you apply for graduation by the scheduled application date. For example, if you want to graduate in May, the application deadline might be in April or even March. If you do not apply in time, you will have to wait until the next graduation to receive your degree, which could be in December of that year. This delay might affect your job searching or your plans to apply to graduate school.
  - o Register with your career center's job listing service so that you can be informed about currently available positions for students in your major.
  - o Check with the career center for information on companies that will be doing interviews on your campus.
  - o Reach out to those friends you made last year in your major. Did they get jobs? If so, where? How hard was it to find that job? Are they satisfied with the job?
  - o Attend a job fair. This time, you're actually trying to get an interview. Come prepared, come professional, and come as yourself. First impressions are very important, so pace yourself and only talk to a representative when you're calm, confident, and ready.

After you graduate, consider joining your university's alumni association. Below is my own personal story about joining an alumni association:

I graduated from Columbia University with my master's degree in 2011, and I knew that being part of a "Columbia University alumni network" would be a great asset. However, I was hesitant to join events because of the membership costs (I already owed enough money for my Ivy League education!) and because I wasn't sure it would be "worth it" in terms of who I would meet and what kinds of relationships I could build. The first alumni event I ever attended was in 2019 at The Peninsula Hotel in Tokyo (a five-star hotel), and the event admission fee was 5,000 Japanese Yen (my lunch budget for two weeks). It was a joint party with alumni from Princeton University and Cornell University. Admittedly, I was more nervous joining this party than I was on my first day of classes at Columbia. I was in a room with architects, engineers, and business managers, all of whom I was sure made much more money than I did and were much better connected than I was. I awkwardly stood around a snack table eating pita chips and drinking pinot grigio, looking at my watch, and thinking about just giving up and leaving. Thankfully, a man walked up to me. He was looking at my nametag that had a blue circle on it, which signified my Columbia alumnus status. He introduced himself, telling me that he also went to Columbia about seven years before I did. We started having a nice conversation about living in New York City and its similarities and differences from Tokyo. Then, when he asked for my Facebook account information, we realized we had a similar friend: his cousin! I met his cousin in New York City when I was a student, and his cousin and I had stayed friends over the years, going out to dinner occasionally. Not only did this one meeting with the association encourage me to stay connected to the friends I had already made while I was a student, but it also smoothly introduced me to new, interesting people with which I had a commonality. I look forward now to attending future events, even though I will have to budget my lunches accordingly so that I have some money saved up for them.

Ultimately, the advising center staff is there to help you safely, efficiently, and effectively cross the bridges that you'll face. Take their advice.

Self-Reflection/Discussion Questions:

1. What kinds of classes are you most looking forward to taking? Which are you least looking forward to?

13. CREDENTIALS, MAJORS, AND REQUIREMENTS

The most common credentials you can earn from colleges and universities are certificates, associate degrees, bachelor's degrees, master's degrees, and doctoral degrees. Other specialty terminal degrees include juris doctorates, medical doctorates, master's of business administration, and more. You do not need a certificate to earn an associate degree, and you do not need an associate degree to earn a bachelor's degree. However, you do need a bachelor's degree before you can earn a master's degree or a doctorate degree. Some graduate school students get accepted into "MA/PhD" programs in which they will earn both degrees, while others might simply get accepted into "PhD" programs that skip over the requirements for earning the master's degree.

The explanation of differences between certificates, associate degrees, and bachelor's degrees below is remixed from the open textbook A Different Road to College, pp. 23-24:

> The main difference between certificates, associate degrees, and bachelor's degrees come down to these five factors: time, tuition, admission requirements, amount of coursework, and career opportunities. A certificate usually means you have completed a specialized form of training. It may demonstrate technical knowledge in a field, and it is generally faster to complete than a degree. Sometimes, a certificate can be a benchmark showing progress toward a degree. An associate degree is commonly referred to as a "two-year" degree. Examples of careers that often minimally require an associate degree include health care professionals, information technologists, and culinary artists. An associate degree will often meet most, if not all, of the general education required classes needed to pursue a bachelor's degree. Some students who complete an associate degree will then transfer to a university to complete a bachelor's degree. A bachelor's degree is commonly referred to as a "four-year" degree, and it requires around 120 credits (or about forty courses) to complete. These numbers vary based on whether the college operates on the quarter or the semester schedule. People working in education, engineering, business, finance, and other fields are often required to obtain a bachelor's degree.

There are two major types of bachelor's degrees: a bachelor's of arts (BA) and a bachelor's of sciences (BS). Before you can earn a bachelor's degree, you must decide on a major. The University of Washington's degree overview website plainly explains that a major is "an extended study of one academic area, usually within one department of the University." Some large public universities (with around 30,000 students), such as The Ohio State University, Purdue University, the University of Minnesota, and Temple University, have around 150 different majors students can choose from.

There are also minors students can pursue in addition to a major. Minors are not full degrees, and the name of your minor study might not be printed on your physical degree. Instead, it shows up on your official university transcript. For example, I received a BA in English, and I completed a minor in Asian studies. My printed degree only lists my degree in English; the information about my Asian studies minor can be found on my official university transcripts.

A somewhat unique feature of United States colleges and universities is that you can pursue more than one major and earn more than one degree simultaneously. For example, if you complete all required courses for a bachelor's in American ethnic studies as well as for a bachelor's in architectural studies, you will receive a single BA degree with "double major" listed on the degree. However, if you complete all required courses for a bachelor's of arts in geography as well as for a bachelor's of sciences in earth and space sciences, you will receive two separate degrees.

You can also choose to take honors classes to graduate "with honors." There are two types of honors at most universities: honors based on grade point average and "university honors." Anyone can graduate with honors if they get good enough grades. Your university will have its own standards for different levels of honors, but the three typical grade point average-based honors are (in Latin and in English): cum laude (with honors), magna cum laude (with high honors), and summa cum laude (with the highest honors). Graduating with "university honors," however, typically requires an additional application procedure and the completion of an honors project. University honors is separate from grade point average-based honors. For example, I graduated from the University of California, Riverside "magna cum laude," and that honor designation is printed on my degree. However, I also received a separate certificate recognizing my "university honors" that bears the title of my honors thesis paper. This "university honors" granted me the rights to wear special cords as graduation regalia. Not every college or university has an honors program. Therefore, if yours does not but you are interested in completing an honors project, contact your dean of academic affairs and ask how an honors program could be created on your campus.

As for graduate students, you can sometimes pursue a concentration or a graduate certificate in a particular field of your degree program. To complete a concentration or graduate certificate, graduate students normally have to take a few extra classes beyond the minimum needed to graduate, or they have to carefully plan all of their classes from their first semester in order to complete the concentration within the standard course hours required. For example, my doctorate in English from the University of Connecticut had graduate certificate options in American studies, digital humanities and media studies, human rights, feminist studies, literary translation, and college instruction.

Generally, students at colleges and universities in the United States must study a wide variety of subjects. In fact, each college or university has a set of required classes that every undergraduate student must take in order to graduate. Regardless of what major you choose, you must pass this set of classes. Many universities will break courses down into "foundational" courses and "breadth" courses. Your school might call them something different, such as Columbia University's infamous "Core Curriculum" and its requirements, but the meaning is essentially the same. Foundational courses are courses all students must satisfy, while breadth courses are requirements with a bit of flexibility in what you choose. "Elective courses" are used to meet graduation requirements but are almost completely your choice. However, electives are not considered part of your "general education" because not everyone is required to take the same types of electives.

For example, Temple University (a large, public university) has four "foundational" course requirements: analytical reading & writing, quantitative literacy, and two courses in "intellectual heritage." All students must satisfy exactly these courses; there are no options or substitutes. However, there are six different types of "breadth" courses: arts, human behavior, race and diversity, world society, science and technology, and US society. Students must take one course in each breadth area except for "science and technology" in which students must take two courses. There are dozens of options that students can pick from that satisfy these breadth requirements. For instance, to satisfy the US society breadth requirement, students could choose to take courses such as "The American Economy," "American Revolutions," "Gender in America," and "The US Constitution and Popular Culture." These courses come from different subjects of study such as American studies, anthropology, economics, geography and urban studies, history, law, sociology, women's studies, and more.

You can learn all about the general education requirements at your college and more in your school's catalog or student handbook (the terms are sometimes used interchangeably and other times very differently). Consider the catalog as an all-encompassing map of the bridges currently established at your institution. Indeed, it is a very important document!

The explanation of college catalogs below is remixed from the open textbook A Different Road to College, pp. 22-23:

> The most important book on campus is the college catalog, or the student handbook. A college catalog is where you can find all the specific details and rules of your school. The purpose is to have all that information in one easy place for prospective students and current students. College catalogs are updated when degree programs, school rules, and student expectations change. Catalogs are usually published each year, so make sure you are looking at the most current one. Specific topics covered include: an overview of the college's history, the availability of financial aid, academic expectations, degree programs and course descriptions, cost estimates for tuition and housing, campus life information, mission statements, statements of faith (for religious institutions), school policies, and student services offered. Most colleges give the general public access to the catalog on the school website. You can also probably pick up a printed copy on campus. However, finding easy-to-use online college catalogs may be frustrating for new college students. Some are complex searchable websites with multiple dropdown windows for selecting parameters, while others are PDF files that are hundreds of pages long. If you ever get frustrated by your school's catalog, visit the welcome center or the admissions office for assistance.

Self-Reflection/Discussion Questions:

1. Do you think colleges and universities should require all students to take "foundational" courses? Why or why not?
2. Are there any subject areas (writing, mathematics, science, etc.) you are nervous about taking in college? Why or why not?
3. Are you interested in pursuing a degree in arts or in sciences? Why?
4. Would you consider double majoring or pursing a double degree? If so, which ones and for what purpose?
5. Is graduating with honors important to you or not? Do you think employers care much about grade point averages?
6. For graduate students, what concentrations or graduate certificates are available in your area of study? Do you think they are worthwhile to complete or not? Why?

14. INSTRUCTORS AND PROFESSORS

AUTHOR'S STORY:

The first graduate student I ever taught was from India. He came to the New Mexico Institute of Mining and Technology, where I was an assistant professor of English, to study petroleum engineering. I was so excited to hear that he would take my technical writing course because I had never taught a graduate student before. He emailed me before the semester began because he wanted to come meet me in my office. I was sitting at my desk when he knocked on the door. I got up, opened it, and I saw him smiling at me. Then, he said, "Hi, Shawn, it's nice to meet you!" and stuck out his hand for a handshake. I shook his hand, but something inside me was immediately disappointed and even a bit angry.

On the surface, this exchange sounds fine, right? However, there was no way that this first-semester graduate student from another country could have known why I was bothered by his greeting. The truth is, in the United States, many professors allow their graduate students to call them by their first names. However, this normally comes after a more formal introduction where the student says, "Hello, Dr. Higgins," and then Dr. Higgins replies, "Oh, no need for that! You're a grad student! Call me Shawn!"

To understand this situation better, let's begin by considering job titles and pronouns.

Job Titles and Pronouns

There are so many possible job titles for people teaching at colleges and universities in the United States. Here is an incomplete list, loosely moving from the lowest level of prestige to the highest:

TEACHING ASSISTANT	Often referred to as a "TA." A TA is a graduate student working for a professor and help-ing them teach their class or run their laboratory.
GRADUATE INSTRUCTOR	This is a graduate student who has some level of autonomy over the courses they teach and those courses' syllabi. A graduate instructor is not helping a professor teach their class. Rather, this class is their own.
VISITING LECTURER	This instructor or professor will only stay at this institution for a few years. Their "visit-ing" status means they are currently employed somewhere else and will return to that institution. It could also mean that the institution has hired them on a fixed short-term contract and does not plan to hire them permanently.
LECTURER OR INSTRUCTOR	These professors can be part-time or full-time, and their positions can be temporary or permanent. They are not on the tenure-track, meaning they are often not required to do research or serve on university committees. They might have doctorate degrees, but they might not. They may teach only one course per term, or they may teach a very full load of courses (four to five) per term.

ADJUNCT PROFESSOR	This term may be the same as "Visiting Lecturer" or "Lecturer" depending on your institution's usage. The difference could be that adjunct professors might have higher degrees (doctorate degrees) than visiting lecturers or instructors, but this is not always true. Most adjunct professors are not on the tenure-track.
VISITING PROFESSOR	This professor will only stay at this institution for a few years. Their "visiting" status means they are currently employed somewhere else and will return to that institution. It could also mean that the institution has hired them on a fixed short-term contract and does not plan to hire them permanently. While "Visiting Lecturer" and "Visiting Professor" may be used interchangeably, a difference could be that visiting professors have higher degrees (doctorate degrees).
ASSISTANT TEACHING PROFESSOR	This professor has a full-time, permanent position that is non-tenure-track. While tenure-track professors are expected to conduct research and serve on university committees as part of their job expectations, assistant teaching professors primarily teach courses, perhaps four to five each semester. They might not ever get "tenure," but that doesn't mean their titles mean anything less.
ASSISTANT PROFESSOR	This professor has a full-time, permanent position that is tenure-track. This is the entry-level title for a professor seeking tenure. Assistant professors are expected to teach classes, conduct research, and serve on academic committees. This rank typically means the professor is in their first one to seven years of their job.
ASSOCIATE PROFESSOR	This professor has a full-time, permanent position. This rank is normally for someone who has been granted tenure and is a middle rank professor. For institutions that prize research among their faculty, earning this rank normally means they have published a book or many academic articles. For institutions that value teaching and service, this rank is for professors who have significantly contributed for more than seven to eight years.
PROFESSOR	This professor has a full-time, permanent position. This is one of the highest ranks a professor can receive and is sometimes referred to as a "full professor." Professors have normally either significantly contributed to their fields by publishing multiple books or multiple articles and are viewed as an expert by others in their field, or they are foundational to the teaching and organization of an institution. Not all assistant or associate professors are guaranteed the rank of "Professor"; it is a title that often must be applied for and can be denied.
PROFESSOR EMERITUS OR EMERITA	This professor is retired or in the process of retiring. Professors emeriti and professors emeritae might teach occasional classes, give occasional lectures, or serve as graduate student committee members and co-advisors. However, they are most likely not working a full-time load at the university anymore.

It's not as simple as calling your professors by their job titles, however. You would never call someone "Graduate Assistant X" or "Assistant Professor Y." Instead, you need to figure out which title they prefer and what level of formality is needed in a given situation. Cultures of formality and collegiality vary widely from country to country and from region to region.

Then, if you take factors such as race, gender, economic class, age, and other biographical attributes into account, how you interact with instructors and professors at your school can be influenced in many confusing and humbling ways. For example, I know many female professors who share stories of not being given their due respect and who attribute that to their gender in their profession. This might be because students are culturally programmed to respect a male professor and will call him "Dr. X" or "Professor X" readily. However, students seem to be comfortable cutting these titles off from a female professor's title, resulting in simply calling her by her family name. Whereas a student might say "Hi, Dr. X!" to a male professor in the hallway, they might then two minutes later say "Hey, Y!" to a female professor. This casualness might be because that student feels more comfortable around Dr. Y because Dr. X intimidates everyone in the department. However, even if that casualness is coming from a positive feeling, the perceived message is that the student might not respect Dr. Y as much as Dr. X.

Here are some recommendations for how to navigate this confusing culture:

1. Ask your instructor or professor for their preference. Some people with doctorate degrees prefer "Dr. Y" at all times. Some young graduate instructors will want you to call them "Professor X" because it carries more power and separates them from their students. Some university professors or professors emeriti who have taught for forty years will prefer you just call them by their first names because, well, they have had enough years of formality and respect.

2. If you don't know your professor's preference and can't find out, use their official title and degree by default. For example, if you know your professor has a doctorate degree because the school website lists them as "Person Y, PhD," then call them "Dr. Y" the first time you meet them. If you aren't sure whether they have a doctorate or not because the website simply lists "Person Y," then call them "Professor Y" when you first meet them. "Professor" is a job title; "Doctor" is a degree earned. Not all professors are doctors, and calling a professor "doctor" when that person doesn't have a doctorate degree might lead to embarrassment.

3. If you don't know your professor's official title or degree, then simply use their entire publicized name. In conversation, you could greet someone by saying their full name (for example, "Shawn Higgins?") and by offering a physical gesture of some sort, like a handshake. In email, you could begin with a salutation and their full name (for example, "Dear Shawn Higgins,").

    a. Avoid using gendered pronouns. There is no need to call someone mister, miss, or missus in conversation or in email. Similarly, avoid sir and madam/ma'am. Do not assume that someone identifies as a man or a woman, especially if you have never met them before.

Outside of attending classes with professors, there are two other important ways you will interact with them: during office hours and when you ask for a letter of recommendation.

Office Hours

Professors "hold office hours" outside of class time to provide students with the opportunity to speak with them privately about a number of issues. Specifically, students can go to ask the professor about general course questions, specific skill or assignment assessment, or for clarification and expansion of topics discussed during class. Beyond this, office hours are a chance to see the "human" side of each other outside of the classroom environment. Professors often reveal much about themselves through the way their offices are arranged and decorated, including the books on their shelves and the degrees or adornments hanging on their walls and on their desks. Conversely, professors can get to know students on an individual basis in office hours.

In order to use office hours effectively, follow these steps:

1. Visit your professor during their scheduled office hours, or make an appointment for an agreed upon time in advance. Try not to show up at their office randomly outside of office hours. Professors are often in their offices preparing for classes, grading, working on research, or maybe just eating their lunches. Even though they are "in," try not to assume that they are always "available." If you show up during their scheduled office hours, however, you have a better chance of being welcomed into their office.

2. Come prepared with a purpose for the visit. Bring a set of specific questions or some notes you took from the lecture that you would like to know more about.

3. For more tips, visit the "Academic Situations and Scripts: In Office Hours" section of this book's appendix.

Letters of Recommendation

When you apply for a scholarship, internship, graduate school, or maybe a job, you will want to ask your professors for a letter of recommendation. Asking for a letter is not a major favor, so don't be scared to ask. However, there are some important considerations to make before asking:

1. Try to ask for a letter from someone who has a permanent position at your university. If you plan to ask someone who was a graduate assistant when they taught you as a first-year student, be careful. They might graduate from their doctoral program and leave the school before you need the letter! Similarly, if you want to ask someone who works as an adjunct professor, you need to make sure they are still employed by your university. They might have left the university for a full-time position somewhere else (hopefully), or they might not have had their contract renewed by your university (unfortunately).

2. Make sure you ask them with enough advance notice of the deadline. How much time is "enough"? There is no set number of days, but I would try to ask at least three weeks in advance. Asking for a letter on Monday for an application due Friday will not give your professor enough time to write a quality, customized letter for you. Every professor who has written letters of recommendation before can easily put together a generic

letter for you. However, some professors will refuse to do this out of consideration for you; generic letters are not very effective when compared with letters from professors that are clearly customized. Ideally, you would ask the professor a month in advance.

3. Make sure you did well enough in that class for the professor to say something positive about you. This does not include just grades; it also includes your participation, your professionalism, and your impact on the class atmosphere. If you got below a B grade in the class, I would not suggest asking for a letter of recommendation. If the professor doesn't seem to remember your name when you talk to them in office hours because you didn't participate much in the class, I would reconsider asking them for a letter. If you received a high grade in the class and the professor remembers your name but you had a negative impact on the class, such as being disruptive or not being a productive group member for assignments, you might want to ask another professor for a letter.

4. Make sure you give that letter writer everything they need to submit the recommendation on time. If they have to submit it to a specific website, make sure you register their email address on the website in advance. If you want them to include specific information about a project you did in their class, give them those details weeks before the deadline so that they can add it to their letter. If the letter should be addressed to a specific person or agency, make sure you give it to them in advance and in the correct format. If you make mistakes with this information, then your letter writers will also make those mistakes. This will not only reflect negatively on your letter writers, making them look unprofessional, but you will probably not be awarded the thing or position to which you are applying as a result.

Self-Reflection/Discussion Questions:

1. Would you prefer to take classes with a younger professor closer to your age and with less experience or an older professor with more experience? Why?
2. What kinds of questions might you ask a professor in office hours that you should not ask during a class session?
3. Are you someone who actively participates in your classes? If not, how can you make sure that your professor notices you in the classroom and remembers your name after the course ends?

15. DIVERSITY, INCLUSION, AND EQUITY

QUOTES FROM THE FIELD:

"Equity and inclusion is not a fixed point; it's not something you either have or you don't. We can apply psychologist Carol Dweck's ideas about growth mindset to the work of equity and inclusion. Having a growth mindset means that we are going to make mistakes and be out of our comfort zones sometimes. Greater equity and inclusion is a goal we can keep working toward. I believe in the principle that we can get better at living and working together in a diverse community. Through faith and collaboration, we can accomplish good things."

—Floyd Cheung, PhD
Vice President for Equity and Inclusion and Professor of English
Language & Literature and American Studies, Smith College

Not everyone's bridge to college is the same length, paved with the same smoothness, or maintained with the same care. Some people find it very hard to locate any bridges at all, in fact. Even when some people try their best to build bridges to academia, it seems like an unidentifiable force on the other side blocks their attempts. Have you ever been discouraged from pursuing certain educational, social, economic, or career opportunities because of who you are? Who you are might mean the color of your skin, your native language, your cultural identity, your economic class, your religious affiliation, your sexual orientation, your gender identification, your physical and mental abilities, and more. If you say "yes" to this question, then you might want to learn about these systems of oppression while you're a college student and ways to undo them. If you say "no" to this question, then it is your duty as an informed and educated college student to learn about the experiences of those who say "yes." It is your duty to learn how to undo the systems of oppression that created this reality.

Many universities have as their stated goals in their mission statements the promotion of "intercultural learning" and of "lifelong learning." Both of these are reflective practices and work toward an awareness of a cultural self. On page 31 of the open textbook Intercultural Learning: Critical Preparation for International Student Travel, the authors define "intercultural learning" as being open to alternative ways of knowing, being in, and seeing the world. Find your institution's mission statement and see if terms such as "intercultural learning" are in it. If so, then diversity, inclusion, and equity should not be considered supplemental or outside parts of your university experience; they should be central.

The following key terms in the below table are important for conversations about diversity, inclusion, and equity and are remixed from the open textbook Intercultural Learning: Critical Preparation for International Student Travel, pp. 36-38. That textbook's authors paraphrased each of these key words from original scholarly sources. I have not included the scholarly sources here for simplicity and because I cannot verify the exact paraphrases done by that textbook's authors. This is not an intentional secondhand plagiarism of those original sources. If you want to find the original sources of these paraphrases and of my own below, please access the references on pages 48-51 of that text.

ACCULTURATION	The process of adopting culture between individuals or groups. Acculturation can be voluntary when you agree to adopt another's culture. Acculturation also can be involuntary when you must accept and participate in another's culture.
ACTIVE LISTENING	Fully concentrating on what is being said rather than passively hearing the message of the speaker. Trying to be neutral and non-judgmental in your listening by avoiding reacting simultaneously.
ALIENATION	The feeling or reality of exclusion, nonbelonging, and separateness.
COLONIALISM	Refers to the event of an alien people invading the territory inhabited by people of a different race and culture to establish political, social, spiritual, intellectual, and economic domination over that territory and people. It includes territorial and resource appropriation by the colonizer and loss of sovereignty by the colonized. The term also refers to a set of beliefs used to legitimize or promote this system, especially the belief that the morals and ethics of the colonizer are superior to those of the colonized.
CRITICAL CONSCIOUSNESS	The ability to perceive social, political, and economic oppression and to act against the oppressive elements of society.
CRITICAL REFLECTION	The transformative process of understanding how power and domination come into practice. Critical reflection includes both structural analysis (such as of class, gender, or race) and cultural factors (such as of values, beliefs, or behaviors).
CROSS-CULTURAL PRACTICE	Practice where there is a diversity of traditions and intergenerational issues, ideologies, beliefs and religions, and race and ethnicities.
CULTURAL COMPETENCE	The ability to successfully form, foster, and improve relationships with members of a culture different from one's own. It aims to avoid cultural blindness, or the assumption that all people are the same. At the same time, it is important not to fall into the trap of believing that there are so many differences that we cannot understand or relate to other people at all. Cultural competence is based on a commitment to actively seek information about different ways of doing things and applying and incorporating this information in practice. An understanding of the values, perceptions, social structure, norms, mores, and verbal and non-verbal communication strategies of other cultures. The process by which individuals and systems respond respectfully and effectively to people of all cultures, languages, classes, races, ethnic backgrounds, religions, and other diversity factors in a manner that recognizes, affirms, and values the worth of individuals, families, and communities and protects and preserves the dignity of each.
CULTURAL GENOCIDE	A term used to describe the deliberate destruction of the cultural heritage of a people or nation for political, military, religious, ideological, ethnical, or racial reasons. Cultural genocide is the purposeful weakening and ultimate destruction of cultural values and practices.

CULTURAL IMPERIALISM	The process whereby imperialist control is aided and abetted by importing supportive forms of culture.
CULTURE	A system of beliefs, values, and customs that are learned, shared, and transmitted through symbols. Cultures continually evolve through internal processes and in contact with the environment and other cultures. Culture is the foundation of all human activities, which derive their meaning and value from it. Cultures are not monolithic structures that exert definable influences over people's values, beliefs, and behaviors. Often influences are subtle, go unrecognized, or exist as a composite of cultural and spiritual values drawn from a variety of sources.
CULTURE SHOCK	The stress, anxiety, or discomfort a person feels when they are placed in an unfamiliar cultural environment, due to the loss of familiar meanings and cues relating to communication and behavior.
ETHNICITY	A sense of group identification with beliefs, values, and customs that are learned, shared, and transmitted through symbols. While race, ethnicity, and nation are often used interchangeably, they are discrete. Race tends to focus on physical attributes or phenotypes such as skin color. Ethnicity refers to a person's origins and association with a specific cultural group. Nation refers to nationality within a nation-state.
ETHNOCENTRISM	A basic attitude expressing the belief that one's own ethnic group or one's own culture is superior to other ethnic groups or cultures, and that one's cultural standards can be applied in a universal manner.
EUROCENTRISM	A view that Europeans are culturally and politically superior to all other peoples in the world.
GLOBALIZATION	The ongoing process that is linking people, neighborhoods, cities, regions, and countries much more closely together than they have ever been before. This has resulted in our lives being intertwined with people in all parts of the world via the rapid distribution of the food we eat, the clothing we wear, the music we listen to, the information we get, and the ideas we hold.
HEGEMONY	Leadership or dominance of one state or social group over another. Nowadays, it is also used to describe the dominant position of a particular set of ideas and their associated tendency to become common sense.
IMPERIALISM	A total system of foreign power in which another culture, people, and way of life penetrate, transform, and come to define the colonized society. A policy of extending a country's power or influence through colonization, military force, economic control, or other means. The term "imperialism" should not be confused with "colonialism." Imperialism operates from the center, it is a state policy, and is developed for ideological as well as financial reasons, whereas colonialism is development for settlement or commercial intentions.

INSTITUTIONAL RACISM	The ways in which racist beliefs or values have been built into the operations of social institutions in such a way to discriminate against, control, and oppress various minority groups. Also known as "systemic racism."
RACE	A highly contentious term that has shifted considerably over time. Scientifically, all human beings belong to the same race, yet historically the meaning of the term "race" has varied. Politically, race is a social construction that changes with the times to meet certain needs of the state or tribe.
RACISM	A set of economic, political, and ideological practices whereby a dominant group exercises hegemony over subordinate groups. Racism has three inter-related, interactive components that are embedded in and negotiated through everyday life: personal, institutional, and cultural.
WESTERN THOUGHT	A way of thinking, a history of philosophy rooted in "rational" thought where the individual subject is highly valued. Secular humanism prevails and the rational, autonomous, freely choosing individual is highly valued. Democracy and freedom of choice is seen as the most just system promoting human rights, social justice, fairness, and equality of opportunity. Neoliberal economics tend to dominate the social terrain. Free market economics and free trade are priorities. The dominant history is that of exploration and conquest, of voyages, of discovery in the interests of progress, and of the development of Western civilizations. Social life is highly bureaucratized, impersonal, and largely individualistic.
WHITE PRIVILEGE	An institutional, rather than personal, set of benefits for those whose race gives them "white skin." Thus, whiteness is a racial identity, and, in most Western societies, it is a default standard against which all other groups of color are compared, contrasted, and made visible.
WORLDVIEW	A way of seeing and understanding the world. It is a philosophy of life. It is a mental framework of ideas and attitudes about the world we live in, people around us, existing beliefs, and ultimately, ourselves in relation to it all. One's worldview is shaped by socioeconomical, cultural, historical, and contemporary happenings. One also acts accordingly to one's values and worldview.

As you work through your college life, take a DIVER approach to critical reflection with regard to various situations and challenges against diversity, equity, and inclusion. DIVER stands for:

- Describe
- Interpret
- Verify
- Explain
- Reconstruct

The explanation in the bulleted list below is remixed from the open textbook Intercultural Learning: Critical Preparation for International Student Travel, pp. 27:

- **Describe:** Listen, observe, and remain open, holding off on judgment or evaluation. Simply describe what you saw and what you heard.
- **Interpret:** Write or discuss what you thought about the situation. Think of two or three different ways your description could be interpreted. Try to put yourself in other peoples' shoes and think about the interpretations they might offer. What does your description reveal about what is important to you? What aspects do you pay less attention to?
- **Verify:** Acknowledge that your culture and the cultures of others are dynamic. Therefore, everyone's understandings need to be constantly checked through collaborative learning processes. Ask others questions to explore your assumptions and interpretations in order to test your understanding.
- **Explain:** Connect your interpretation with theories and concepts that you've learned about. Where might your assumptions come from? What does your description reveal about your values, beliefs, or awareness of power? What does this tell you about your cultural self and others' cultural practices?
- **Reconstruct:** Put these steps back together. What does this mean for yourself and your future professional practice? What might you do differently in the future? What new understandings about yourself and others do you bring to a situation?

16. RIGHTS AND RESPONSIBILITIES

There are federal laws that protect the rights of students, staff, and faculty members of United States colleges and universities. These are your barriers, your safeguards, and your patrol officers helping you safely across the bridge toward graduation. Here are some of the most important terms and resources you should know about:

- FERPA
    o The Family Educational Rights and Privacy Act (FERPA) is a federal law that gives parents or legal guardians the right to access their child's education records. These rights include having records corrected/changed when needed as well as controlling what kinds of personally identifiable information can be shared. These records include information such as grades, transcripts, class lists, student course schedules, health records (at the K-12 level), financial information (at the college or university level), and student discipline files. However, once a child turns eighteen years old or once a child of any age enters a college or university, parents no longer have these rights; only the student will have access to their own education records. Students can often submit an educational release of records form that lists specific people (including their parents) who are allowed to access their information. However, submitting this form is optional; a university student's information is private by default.

- Office of Civil Rights
    o The United States Department of Education's Office of Civil Rights (OCR) has many responsibilities to protect students. Four of the most critical areas in which the OCR protects students include discrimination against race/color/national origin, against a person's sex, against people with disabilities, and against people of certain ages. In schools, libraries, museums, or other educational programs that receive federal funding, discriminating against any of these groups is against federal civil rights laws. Key issue areas include recruitment, admissions, counseling, financial aid, athletics, discipline, and employment. These key issue areas are identified using the following terms:

        - Title VI, or "Title Six": Title VI specific key issue areas include racial harassment, school segregation, and denial of language services to English learners.
        - Title IX, or "Title Nine": Title IX specific key issue areas include sex-based harassment, failure to provide equal opportunity in athletics, discrimination in a school's science/technology/engineering/math (STEM) courses and programs, discrimination against pregnant and parenting students, and single-sex education.

17. MORE QUOTES FROM THE FIELD

I asked some of my colleagues at different institutions to answers some questions about their experiences in college and after. I think students should talk to as many graduates, faculty, and staff members as possible to get a sense of what you might expect in college. Many of my colleagues shared reactions or responses to these questions. Instead of listing them individually with all of their answers, I combined them here for the sake of brevity. Remember that every professor and staff member you meet has probably been where you are right now. We know what it was like to be a student. These replies below are full of wisdom – read carefully!

Participants:

- Patrick S. Lawrence, Assistant Professor of English, University of South Carolina Lancaster
- George Miller, Associate Dean for Academic Affairs, Temple University, Japan Campus
- Lata Murti, Associate Professor of Sociology, Brandman University's Online Campus
- Mark Padoongpatt, Associate Professor of Asian American Studies and Interdisciplinary Studies, University of Nevada, Las Vegas
- Eleanor Reeds, Assistant Professor of English, Hastings College
- Sarajean Rossitto, Lecturer in Political Science, Temple University, Japan Campus
- Nitasha Sharma, Associate Professor of African American Studies and Asian American Studies, Northwestern University
- Casey terHorst, Associate Professor of Biology, California State University, Northridge
- Caroline Kieu Linh Valverde, Associate Professor of Asian American Studies, University of California, Davis

I wish more students who applied to college knew that . . .

- It's good to be "still deciding" on your major area of study.
- Universities have turned increasingly corporate. You may not get the experience or the return on your investment that you hoped for.
- Your education just starts in the classroom. It then continues around campus, across the city, and around the world.
- You need to take initiative. The key thing is what you put into your college experience, not your grades.
- The admissions system is racist and classist and misogynistic. If you're not admitted, it's not a reflection of who you are. However, it's important to know that this is the system (although it's slowly changing), and you have to know the rules to play the game. If you're able to get in the game, fix the system from within.
- You will probably change your major at least once, if not several times, during your undergraduate career. This is completely normal. It is part of self-exploration, finding your passion, and expanding your mind and possibilities.
- We expect you to grow from being a consumer of research and knowledge to a produc-

er. In the first couple of years, you should be a sponge: soak up and consume as much knowledge and information as you can in lower-division courses. Just learn and learn. Then, when you start to take upper-division courses, especially in your major, you'll be expected to shift to questioning existing knowledge and producing your own insights.

- It's not always necessary to attend the most elite and expensive universities. State universities can teach you lessons on perseverance and initiative in ways that private and small colleges do not.
- Whether you get into your "dream" school or the last one on your list, remember there are so many factors shaping a college experience.

On the first day of class, students should try to . . .

- Enjoy the excitement and not worry too much about making an impression on your professors or peers.
- Connect with your professors and classmates. Community will be the best aid to your learning.
- Read and understand syllabi policies.
- Compare the schedules for all your classes so you can plan ahead for deadlines.
- Enjoy lectures, think critically, and take in the whole experience of being a new college student.
- Ask questions and talk to people you don't know.
- Have a one-minute conversation with your professors to tell them who you are and why you're taking their class. This is especially important in large classes where it's easy to get lost in the crowd.
- Sit at the front of the class and study the syllabus.
- If it's a smaller class (less than forty), introduce yourself to the professor if they seem approachable.
- Give themselves a break. Just soak it in and don't feel too overwhelmed.

I want to tell all college students that . . .

- The habits of mind that college trains you in are underappreciated and overlooked.
- The most valuable learning takes place when you are open to going outside of your comfort zone.
- College can be very hard socially and psychologically.
- It's okay to make mistakes. The key thing is to learn from your errors and keep trying new things.
- You can change majors, and you can enter fields of employment beyond your major after you graduate.
- College should be enjoyable.
- Studying is a team sport.
- You should pursue studies that you feel passionate about.
- College is the time to find "your people." We grow up influenced by our families

that were assigned to us at birth. Find the people who you identify with the most, who understand you the best, and who will become your new chosen family. When you find that group, listen to them and let them influence who you are, and, in turn, influence them.

- The "little things" go a long way. For example, reading and studying the syllabus will help debrief you on what to expect in lectures. Visiting office hours regularly and coming prepared with questions about your professors' research interests will help you better understand their approach to the world.

- When it comes to choosing a major, there are two ways to think about it: focus on a career, or focus on a skillset. Remember that your major will not guarantee you a job in a particular area. For instance, earning a BA in business will not guarantee you can open up your own business; a BA in psychology does not guarantee you will be a psychologist. Instead, think about majors in terms of the skillset you want to have to make sense of the world.

- You should do the required readings! The professor assigned them for a reason!

- These may be the best or the worst years of your life, but they are a finite amount of time and after that, you will be out of college. Try to make the best of it. This does NOT mean attempting to do everything and being involved in every organization on campus. It does not mean you have to triple major or gear yourself toward a lucrative post-college career. It DOES mean you should learn who you are as a person: what are the preferred rhythms of your daily life? What kinds of peer groups do you thrive in? How do you deal with difficult circumstances? This is a time of growth – mental, emotional, and physical.

I have a specific message for . . .

- All students!
  - It is imperative to take classes in ethnic and racial studies. No other fields will teach you about power, history, and inequality in quite the same ways.
- Asian American students!
  - This is a great time to learn about your racial/ethnic identity and its relation/impact to the university, community, state, country, and world.
- Female students!
  - Don't be afraid to speak up and own your perspective or idea. Nothing is more disheartening to me as a professor than clever, diligent, and kind young women who don't know their own worth: have confidence in what you have to offer.
  - Be equal. Don't be afraid of risks or of being aggressive because you can't succeed without these things. Never play the victim card.
- First-Generation students!
  - Knowing how to succeed in college can be mysterious. When you struggle, you'll see others succeeding. You might assume you don't belong there. What you don't see is that some people succeed because they asked their parents or their older sibling or somebody else in the family how to do well. They know the rules, the

secret tips, and the insider info. Although college faculty members try to provide some of this secret info to students, we are wildly bad at it. We assume students know what they need to do. But if nobody has ever told you, how could you possibly know? One way to solve this is to ask questions. If your friend is doing well in the class, ask them how they study. If you don't understand something in class, more than likely, the professor didn't explain it well enough. Follow up with them after class or in office hours. Office hours are your time with the professor. You're not a burden. Their job is to help you do well in the course. Go to office hours and ask them how, and then try do something different. Success in a college course requires different skills than you needed in high school. You have to study how to learn at a different level. Knowledge about those skills is out there, but, unfortunately, it won't be handed to you; you have to go seek it out.

o   Don't be afraid to claim your identity as a first-generation college student. Embrace it. If you have trouble or have questions, tell your professors and/or friends that you are a first-generation student and don't know how college is supposed to work. It is not your fault. You are a trailblazer and a pioneer.

- International students!
  o   Explain the challenges of your situation to professors. Find at least one professor who also worked and lived internationally to advocate for you! We're out there, I promise.
- Online learning students!
  o   The first time I meet my students in person is at their graduation ceremony. Yet, often, we greet each other warmly, as if we have known each other for years. And we have, virtually. I teach undergraduate sociology classes completely online. I must connect with my students and get to know them. I must also allow them to get to know me, without the help of facial expressions, hand gestures, posture, or tone of voice—all the non-verbal language that study after study says makes up most of our communication with others. How do I do this? I choose my words carefully and intentionally to let students know I care not only about their learning, but also about them. Rather than writing, "Why haven't you been submitting assignments?" when emailing a student, I write, "I hope this message finds you well. I notice that you haven't submitted any assignments during the last two weeks. Is everything okay?" The extra words are worth it. So is asking my students a lot of questions instead of telling them what to do. When giving them feedback while grading their assignments, I ask, "Could you have explained the point you made in this paragraph further?" instead of just writing "incomplete" or "insufficient." Words matter. Especially when interacting completely online. My words are what my students carry with them. They determine whether a student has a positive or a negative learning experience in my fully online courses. A positive experience motivates my students to continue learning about the course subject matter beyond the eight-week term. A negative experience may cause students to feel that they are incapable of understanding the course subject matter. If that happens, they might not try to learn more about it after the course ends.

I strive to give all of my students positive online learning experiences—the kind that lead to warm greetings at graduations even though we have never met before.

- Sexual minorities!
  o If you have not yet been able to be yourself or who you think you are, this is the time to just be you.
- Students of color!
  o Seek out professors you feel you can trust. Lean on them; turn to them in moments of doubt. Take ethnic studies courses so that you can study issues of race, racism, inequality, sexism, and more. These will help you better understand yourself and your place and power in the world.

One key attribute I think all successful college students share is . . .

- An optimistic determination that they will succeed.
- Curiosity.
- They are willing to take feedback and to grow.
- A motivation to learn.
- Openness.
- They participate in campus life. Join a club or spend time with friends on campus.
- They find ways to care about course content, and they connect it to their own experiences.
- A desire for attending to the world's problems.

What really got me through college was . . .

- Professors that I trusted.
- THERAPY. GO TO THERAPY.
- My friends.
- Working on what I was truly interested in.
- My mission in life.
- Finding my intellectual passion.
- My amazing mentors. As a first-generation student of color, I turned to professors of color. I visited them during office hours, read their books/articles, and took classes with them. I was also an out-of-state student at a predominately white school, so building a tight-knit community with other students of color and working with professors of color really got me through college.
- My flexibility, my lack of obsession about grades, and my active social life.

After you finish college, please remember . . .

- Your college is a lifelong support system. Your teachers, classmates, and the academic staff will be there for you, always.

- Return to campus and share your knowledge with the next wave of students.
- You are responsible for articulating the value of your degree.
- The perfect career is one you make for yourself by showing what you can do when given the opportunity.
- Your possibilities are as wide as the ocean.
- No one really cares what grades you got (except grad school admissions).
- Be tough and don't be afraid of risk.
- Apply lessons of social justice and finances to real life.
- Stay in touch with professors you loved and/or ones who cared about you.

Appendix

Photo by Shawn Higgins

Appendix

18. TWENTY ACADEMIC JARGON WORDS YOU MIGHT NEED TO KNOW

This list does not follow the exact order or recommendations of other word lists, such as Averil Coxhead's Academic Word List (AWL). Instead, it is a simple collection of my own recommendations as a teacher of writing and literature who has taught in large state universities, science and technical universities, and in United States universities abroad. For each word, I include not a definition but instead a kind of usage guide or the context in which that word might appear in your academic life. For good, clear definitions of these words and phrases, visit Merriam-Webster's Learner's Dictionary.

1. "Account for"
   a. You might need to "account for" bias, variables, or factors when completing your analysis of something. This means think about, consider, plan for, and explain.
   b. If you are asked to "account for" something odd, troubling, or problematic (see number eighteen in this list), you should try to explain why it exists. It probably contradicts or complicates something else that author/speaker has written/said.

2. "Ambiguous"
   a. Texts can be "ambiguous," meaning that they cannot easily be defined in a singular way. Your task is to recognize this ambiguity and to analyze it, not necessarily to force it into a clear, singular definition. When discussing artistic creations, "ambiguous" tends to have a positive connotation.
   b. Your writing or explanation might be "ambiguous," meaning that a reader/audience cannot easily determine your point or argument. In this case, you should try to clarify and strengthen your statement. When discussing student writing, "ambiguous" tends to have a negative/critical connotation.

3. "Attribute"
   a. When discussing an effect (for example, a decline of the American economy), a professor might ask you, "What can we attribute this to?" or "And what does the author of our text attribute this to?" This is asking you to identify the cause for that effect.
   b. In citations, works cited entries, and bibliographies, you will be asked to "attribute" quotes and paraphrases accurately and honestly. This means you must give credit to a source or document your research. Students who forget to include proper citations such as quotation marks or parenthetical information might receive a comment asking, "Are you attributing this to anyone?"

4. "Commentary"
   a. Many students wonder if instructors want to know what their opinion is about readings or topics. The answer is "yes," but most often only if your opinion is "informed," meaning that you know something about the readings or the topic. For example, an assignment might ask you to "provide commentary" on how the author of a text builds their argument. The instructor here is not asking for your simple reactions or quick thoughts. Instead, "commentary" is a synonym for "explanation" or maybe even "analysis."

5. "Component"

   a. Many university assignments are made up of multiple "components," meaning there are several small related tasks all tied together as one assignment. Sometimes these components are graded separately, but other times a singular assignment might have multiple components that are all necessary for the assignment to be considered "complete." For example, the components of a drafted essay might include a brain-storming activity, an outline, a first draft, a revision, an office hour meeting, and a final draft. Each assignment is clearly different, but they are all components of a larger assignment. In a different example, a final exam essay question might have three components: summarize a reading passage, evaluate the author's claims, and forward the author's ideas using your own arguments on the subject. To succeed on this final exam, you must complete all three components.

6. "Concise"

   a. Longer is not always better for academic writing purposes. In fact, if you write unnecessary information or use more words than needed to convey your ideas, you might lose points on university assignments. Professors call these kinds of words "filler." If an assignment prompt asks you to "Write a concise and well-organized essay on X," take that word "concise" seriously; make every word you write impor-tant. If the assignment asks for 500–600 words for that "concise" response, 500 words with no filler will often get you a higher grade than 600 words that includes 100 words of filler.

7. "Concrete"

   a. Concrete support or concrete analysis refers to something connected to numbers or provable facts. If you offer your analysis of an issue in a text and your professor asks for some "concrete support," you should include a direct quote from the text or some data presented in the text that can support your analysis.

8. "Context"

   a. In many academic subjects (and in life generally), context is crucial. In your composition and literature courses, instructors will ask you to quote from texts that you write about. However, you cannot simply find a good quote and insert it into your essay. Before and after doing so, you need to establish the context for the quote or the situation or reasoning from which that quote came. This might be done by summarizing prior events, paraphrasing the setup for a major argumentative claim, or by positioning (see number seventeen in this list) an author against other contemporary scholars writing on the same subject. Similarly, in subjects such as anthropology or political science, many students are eager to analyze actions based on their own systems of belief. However, your professors will advise you to take context into account (see number one in this list). Only by considering the context can you effectively analyze a situation or a line of reasoning.

9. "Credible"

   a. Authors and sources need to be credible to be used in academic research. The author should be an expert in the subject on which they are writing. This doesn't mean they need a university degree or a certification; they must be highly knowledgeable about their subject. Sources also need to be credible, meaning they should be up to date, should not edit authors in ways that distort (see number ten on this list) their meaning, and should fact-check their authors who do not have a high level of credibility.

10. "Distort"

a. In science or mathematics, you might distort your findings or results by not calculating correctly, not accounting for (see number one in this list) variables, or by exaggerating an interpretation (see number sixteen in this list) of your results.

b. In working with texts, you might distort an author's opinion or argument, particularly when you are summarizing or paraphrasing that text.

c. Texts might also distort the way we normally view an issue. This kind of distortion can be appreciated if the issue is normally seen through one dominant history or mode of analysis.

11. "Elaborate"

a. A professor might ask you to "elaborate" on a text. This means you should give your explanation of its themes, symbols, or issues.

b. After you give an answer in class, your professor might ask you to "elaborate" on what you said. This means you should further explain and possibly offer some examples that others can understand.

12. "Explore"

a. If an essay or assignment prompt asks you to "explore" an issue or theme in a text, you should try to present all of the different sides or options or parts of that thing. For example, a prompt asks you to "explore how music and singing function in Harriet Beecher Stowe's Uncle Tom's Cabin." To complete this assignment, you would find all of the places in the text where that thing happens, identify how it functions in the story, and you would then present all of your findings in organized paragraphs. In an exploration, you might not have a clear argument or thesis statement. Instead, you are showing that you understand how complex a thing is.

13. "Framework"

a. If a concept is singular, then a "framework" is a collection of concepts that help build a frame. Once a writer has a frame of concepts, they can continue to build upon it with their own ideas. Your professors might ask you to discuss an author's particular framework. In doing so, you would try to identify all of the various concepts they weave together to build their frame. Similarly, if your professor suggests that your research project needs a more solid framework, they are telling you to make your research based on a more integrated and complete set of concepts. Perhaps you are relying too heavily on just one concept. Instead, you will need to strengthen your frame by making it more of a "work" and not just something made from a single piece or source.

14. "Hypothesis"

a. This term is not widely used in the humanities. Instead, it is used in the sciences to identify an idea or theory that hasn't been proven but does lead to further thinking, questioning, or discussion. In a humanities class, unless your topic is of a scientific nature, it would be strange in your thesis statement to write: "My hypothesis is X."

15. "Infer"

a. "Inferring" is a great skill to practice. However, when you are doing textual analysis, sometimes inferring can get you into trouble. If your assignment asks you to analyze particular quotes within a particular context, you cannot simply infer additional information about the characters, the plot, or the themes of the narrative. Instead, you should stick to what is written and not bring in any assumptions beyond those words.

16. "Interpret"

a. Everyone might "interpret" the meaning of a poem or the ending of a play or the moral of a story differently. And you might have heard some people say that there is "no wrong interpretation" of art. However, some interpretations are better than others. In fact, not all interpretations can be easily accepted. Your interpretation comes from the way the words of the story or the images you see connect with your own personal experience and how you perceive the world. When you share this interpretation with others, you need to help them see things the way you do. If you are unable to make these connections with your audience, they will have a hard time accepting your interpretation. If your interpretation is not grounded in personal experience nor in commonly shared views of the world, then it will be extremely difficult for others to understand how your interpretation makes sense in this context.

17. "Position"

a. Writers have to "position" themselves with, between, and against other writers. When you analyze a non-fiction text, that text's author probably agrees with certain others in their field and disagrees with more. If you analyze a character in a story, that character has probably positioned themselves to defend someone while attacking another. You yourself as a writer must show that you understand your position; you do not exist alone in your thoughts about a subject. You should show that you know who you agree with and that you know who is against you. You must consciously position yourself within the conversation that precedes your ideas and that will undoubtedly continue after your ideas are shared.

18. "Problematic"

a. "Problems" are not bad; they give us an opportunity to rethink things and come up with solutions. However, when a professor says that a text is "problematic" or that someone's reading of a text is "problematic," most often they mean there is something bad about it.

19. "Signpost"

a. Imagine trying to walk a mile or a few kilometers through a metropolitan city using a navigation app. You type in your destination, but when the app gives you your route, there is only one step: "walk until you reach your destination." The route has turns and stops, but the app simply tells you to walk. You would be confused and frustrated, wouldn't you? Similarly, when you write an essay, you need to tell your reader about the smaller steps and stops along the way to your ultimate destination.

This signaling process is called "signposting." When you signpost, you tell your reader what is coming up next, what follows that, what further follows, and what comes after that before arriving at the final destination. You do this in the thesis statement, in the topic sentences of paragraphs, and in the transition sentences of paragraphs. By letting your reader know where they are going before they start walking, they feel more comfortable. And by planning the route in advance, you as the guide feel more comfortable. Instead of just saying where you will arrive by the end of the essay, signpost and tell your reader all of the important stops you will make along the way to the ultimate destination.

20. "Summarize"

a. When you "summarize" a text, your job is to pick out the important information for your usage and then to accurately and adequately restate that information in your own words. A summary is not the same as a quotation. When you summarize, you must take the information into your head, process it, and then re-present it in your own way. Summarizing well is an important skill to learn. Bad summaries can result in two major problems: inaccurate information and plagiarism questions.

19. GRAMMAR FOR COMPOSITION RESOURCES AND REVIEW

DID YOU KNOW?

General education course instructors might base points for some assignments on grammatical accuracy. For example, even if your political science class research paper on foreign worker policies in South Korea is perfectly researched and well thought-out, if you have grammar mistakes, some instructors might lower your grade. Even worse (and unfairly), the instructor might not make this policy clear on their syllabus. To avoid unfortunate situations like this, you should always do your best to write accurately and purposefully.

In college, you will talk about writing. You will read fiction and nonfiction for classes, and you will analyze these pieces of writing in classroom conversations. You will do peer review activities where you read other students' papers and they read yours, after which you will discuss each other's writing. You will meet with your professors to discuss written assignments you're working on, or will meet with them to discuss the grade you got on a written assignment you submitted. If you visit your campus' writing center (you should), you will be paired with a writing center staff member who will talk with you about your writing. In order to do any of these things effectively, you have to know *how to talk about writing*. One of the most fundamental English language topics you can talk about is grammar.

The following statement on talking about writing comes from Dr. Kristina Reardon, who is the associate director for the Center of Writing at the College of the Holy Cross:

"I sometimes hear students on campus say they are afraid to visit the writing center. They worry the tutors will judge them or, worse, that their professors will think they are not good students because they need help with their writing. However, all writers—including famous, published writers—get feedback from readers and work through multiple drafts. In fact, going to a writing center is a sign of strength as a writer, not a sign of weakness. Visiting the writing center shows that you care about your writing. Writing is meant to be read, and it is almost impossible to be both a writer and an objective reader. Have you ever reread a paper several times and thought it looked pretty good, but you learn later that your eyes were deceiving you? An outsider, like a tutor, can offer you their perspective as a reader and help you see your own work more clearly. They can tell you where they were confused as they read but also where they thought your points made sense. They can help you figure out what to add, what you might want to delete, what could be rearranged, and what to rewrite. A good writing center will feature tutors that work with you on your writing. You'll have a conversation. Tutors will ask you questions, such as, "what were you trying to say in certain sections of your writing?," and you'll get a chance to respond. Tutors will not try to push their ideas on you, and they will not edit your work for you. So visit your writing center prepared to have a lively conversation that could change the way you think about your writing and your writing process. The writing process feels isolating when you're just sitting with your computer in a quiet room. Talking about your ideas with someone else, especially when that person is not grading you, can help your ideas mature and your arguments develop. A willingness to share your work with others and to learn and grow through collaboration is truly what makes good students."

The resources and review below will help you think about how to write well for academic purposes.

Resources:

- Azar Grammar: Betty Azar and her co-author Stacy Hagen are renowned for their grammar workbook series, including the books *Basic English Grammar, Fundamentals of English Grammar,* and *Understanding & Using English Grammar.* For college-level writers, I recommend buying *Understanding & Using English Grammar* if you want a rigorous textbook from which to learn and practice. Betty Azar's website has additional activities that are free to download:
  o Vocabulary Worksheets—Beginning Level
  o Vocabulary Worksheets—Intermediate Level
  o Vocabulary Worksheets—Advanced Level
- *Brehe's Grammar Anatomy*: Steven Brehe's book is available as an open textbook that anyone can download. It is a great, easy-to-understand, and in-depth textbook for studying grammar. It comes with an answer key for all exercises at the end as well.
- Purdue University's Online Writing Lab (OWL): You will hear many instructors, writing lab tutors, and fellow students mention this site. It's amazing, and you should definitely get familiar with it. However, it is rather large, and it can be hard to navigate. Therefore, here are some pages that might be of interest. Feel free to search through more pages using the left-hand toolbar once you're on the site.
  o General Writing Resources
  o Rhetorical Situations
  o Understanding Writing Assignments
  o Essay Writing
  o Sample Papers
  o Invention: Starting the Writing Process
  o Developing Strong Thesis Statements
  o Using Logic
  o On Paragraphs
  o Concision
  o Appropriate Language: Overview
  o Key Concepts for Writing in North American Colleges
  o Tips for Writing in North American Colleges
  o Audience Considerations for ESL Writers
  o Using Foreign Languages in Academic Writing in English
  o Plagiarism and ESL Writers
  o ESL Exercises

The review information below is a remix from the open textbook *College ESL Writers: Applied Grammar and Composing Strategies for Success* (2018) by Barbara Hall and Elizabeth Wallace. Key words for further study are in bold the first time I mention them. I've only selected a few areas where I think review would benefit many kinds of writers. This is an incomplete remix of Hall and Wallace's book. Please download it and work through it entirely if you need extra practice on subjects such as outlining, doing peer review, commonly confused words, spelling, word choice, punctuation, capitalization, or an overview of English grammar.

Components of a Sentence

Clearly written, complete sentences require key information: a **subject**, a **verb**, and a full idea. A sentence needs to make sense on its own. Sometimes, complete sentences are also called **independent clauses**. A **clause** is a group of words that may make up a sentence. An independent clause is a group of words that may stand alone as a complete, grammatically correct thought. The following sentences show independent clauses <u>underlined once</u>.

<u>We went to the store</u>. <u>We bought the ingredients on our list</u>, and then <u>we went home</u>.

All complete sentences have at least one independent clause. You can identify an independent clause by reading it on its own and looking for the subject and the verb.

Subjects

When you read a sentence, look for the subject or what the sentence is about. The subject usually appears at the beginning of a sentence as a noun or a pronoun. A noun is a word that identifies a person, place, thing, or idea. A pronoun is a word that replaces a noun. Common pronouns are "I," "he," "she," "it," "you," "they," and "we." In the following sentences, the subject is <u>underlined once</u>.

<u>Malik</u> is the project manager for this project. <u>He</u> will give us our assignments.

In these sentences, the subject is a person: "Malik." The pronoun "He" replaces and refers back to "Malik."

The <u>computer lab</u> is where we will work. It will be open twenty-four hours a day.

In the first sentence, the subject is a place: "computer lab." In the second sentence, the pronoun "It" substitutes for "computer lab" as the subject.

Prepositional Phrases

Many sentences have more than one noun or pronoun in them. You may encounter a group of words that includes a **preposition** with a noun or a pronoun. Prepositions connect a noun, pronoun, or verb to another word that describes or modifies that noun, pronoun, or verb. Common prepositions include "in," "on," "at," "under," "near," "by," "for," "with," and "about." A group of words that begin with a preposition is called a prepositional phrase. A **prepositional phrase** begins with a preposition, and the **object** of that preposition is a noun. It cannot act as the subject of a sentence. The following underlined phrases are examples of prepositional phrases.

> We went <u>on a business trip</u>. That restaurant <u>with the famous pizza</u> was on the way.
> We stopped <u>for lunch</u>.

Verbs

Once you locate the subject of a sentence, you can move on to the next part of a complete sentence: the verb. A verb is often an **action word** that shows what the subject is doing. A verb can also link the subject to a describing word. There are three types of verbs that you can use in a sentence: **action verbs**, **linking verbs**, or **helping verbs**.

A verb that connects the subject to an action is called an action verb. An action verb answers the question: *what is the subject doing?* In the following sentences, the <u>underlined words</u> are action verbs.

> The dog <u>barked</u> at the jogger.
> He <u>gave</u> a short speech before we ate.

A verb can often connect the subject of the sentence to a describing word. This type of verb is called a linking verb because it links the subject to a describing word. In the following sentences, the <u>underlined words</u> are linking verbs.

> The coat <u>was</u> old and dirty.
> The clock <u>seemed</u> broken.

If you have trouble telling the difference between action verbs and linking verbs, remember that an action verb shows that the subject is doing something, whereas a linking verb simply connects the subject to another word that describes or modifies the subject. A few verbs can be used as either action verbs or linking verbs.

> Action Verb: The boy <u>looked</u> for his gloves.
> Linking Verb: The boy <u>looked</u> tired.

Although both sentences use the same verb, the two sentences have completely different meanings. In the first sentence, the verb describes the boy's action. In the second sentence, the verb describes the boy's appearance.

A third type of verb you may use as you write is a helping verb. Helping verbs are verbs that are used the main verb to describe a **mood** or **tense**. Helping verbs are usually a form of "be," "do," or "have." The word "can" is also used as a helping verb. In the following sentences, the verb is <u>underlined once</u> and the helping verb is **<u>underlined bold</u>**.

The restaurant **is** <u>known</u> for its variety of dishes.
She **does** <u>speak up</u> when prompted in class.
We **have** <u>seen</u> that movie three times.
She **can** <u>tell</u> when someone walks on her lawn.

Whenever you write or edit sentences, keep the subject and verb in mind. As you write, ask yourself these questions to keep yourself on track:

Subject: Who or what is the sentence about?
Verb: Which word shows an action or links the subject to a description?

Sentence Structure

Now that you know what makes a complete sentence (a subject and a verb) you can use other **parts of speech** to build on this basic structure. Good writers use a variety of **sentence structures** to make their work more interesting.

Six basic subject-verb patterns can enhance your writing. A sample sentence is provided for each pattern. As you read each sentence, take note of where each part of the sentence falls. Notice that some sentence patterns use action verbs and others use linking verbs.

1. "<u>Subject</u>–<u>Verb</u>": <u>Computers</u> <u>hum</u>.
2. "<u>Subject</u>–<u>Linking Verb</u>–Noun": <u>Computers</u> <u>are</u> tools.
3. "<u>Subject</u>–<u>Linking Verb</u>–Adjective": <u>Computers</u> <u>are</u> expensive.
4. "<u>Subject</u>–<u>Verb</u>–Adverb": <u>Computers</u> <u>calculate</u> quickly.
5. "<u>Subject</u>–<u>Verb</u>–**Direct Object**": <u>Sally</u> <u>rides</u> a **motorcycle**.
6. "<u>Subject</u>–<u>Verb</u>–**Indirect Object**–Direct Object": <u>My coworker</u> <u>gave</u> **me** the reports.

Collective Nouns

One issue with **collective nouns** is that writers sometimes want to use a **plural verb** with them. However, even though they suggest more than one person, they are usually considered singular. Common collective nouns include "audience," "band," "class," "committee," "company," "faculty," "family," "government," "group," "jury," "public," "school," "society," and "team."

The pronouns you use must **agree** with the nouns to which they refer.

Incorrect: Lara's <u>company</u> will have <u>their</u> annual picnic next week.
Correct: Lara's <u>company</u> will have <u>its</u> annual picnic next week.

Sentence Combining: Conjunctive Adverbs

You can join two independent clauses with related and equal ideas together with a **conjunctive adverb** and a **semicolon**. A conjunctive adverb is a linking word that shows a relationship between two clauses. Read the following sentences:

Original sentences: Bridget wants to take part in the next Olympics. She trains every day.

Since these sentences contain two equal and related ideas, they may be joined using a conjunctive adverb. Now, read the revised sentence:

Revised sentence: Bridget wants to take part in the next Olympics; therefore, she trains every day.

The revised sentence explains the relationship between Bridget's desire to take part in the next Olympics and her daily training. Notice that the conjunctive adverb comes after a semicolon that separates the two clauses and is followed by a comma.

Here is a chart of some common conjunctive adverbs with examples of how to use them. Using these occasionally can help you diversify your sentence structure.

FUNCTION	CONJUNCTIVE ADVERB	EXAMPLE
Addition	also, furthermore, moreover, besides	Alicia was late for class and stuck in traffic; furthermore, her shoe heel had broken, and she had forgotten her lunch.
Comparison	similarly, likewise	Recycling aluminum cans is beneficial to the environment; similarly, reusing plastic bags and switching off lights reduces waste.

Function	Conjunctive Adverb	Example
Contrast	instead, however, conversely	Most people do not walk to work; instead, they drive or take the train.
Emphasis	namely, certainly, indeed	The Siberian tiger is a rare creature; indeed, there are fewer than five hundred left in the wild.
Cause and Effect	accordingly, consequently, hence, thus	I missed my train this morning; consequently, I was late for my meeting.
Time	finally, next, subsequently, then	Tim crossed the barrier, jumped over the wall, and pushed through the hole in the fence; finally, he made it to the station.

When writing an essay or a report, don't use too many of these coordinators. The best kind of writing, whether it be academic or professional, is clear and concise. Therefore, only join two clauses that are logically connected and can work together to make one main point. If you repeat the same coordinating conjunction several times in a sentence, you are probably including more than one idea. This may make it difficult for readers to pick out the most important information in each sentence.

Sentence Combining: Subordination

Subordination is used to join two sentences with related ideas by merging them into a **main clause** (a complete sentence) and a **dependent clause** (a construction that relies on the main clause to complete its meaning). This creates a complex sentence. Coordination allows a writer to give equal weight to the two ideas that are being combined, and subordination enables a writer to emphasize one idea over the other. Read the following sentences:

Original sentences: Farnaz stopped to help the injured man. She would be late for work.

To show that these two ideas are related, we can rewrite them as a single sentence using the **subordinating conjunction** "even though."

Revised sentence: Even though Farnaz would be late for work, she stopped to help the injured man.

In the revised version, we now have an independent clause ("she stopped to help the injured man") that stands as a complete sentence and a dependent clause ("even though Farnaz would be late for work") that is subordinate (less important/powerful) to the main clause. The revised sentence emphasizes the fact that Farnaz stopped to help the injured man, rather than the fact she would be late for work. We could also write the sentence this way:

Revised sentence 2: Farnaz stopped to help the injured man even though she would be late for work.

The meaning remains the same in both sentences, with the subordinating conjunction "even though" introducing the dependent clause.

To punctuate sentences correctly, look at the position of the main clause and the subordinate clause. If a subordinate clause is before the main clause, use a comma. If the subordinate clause follows the main cause, no punctuation is required.

Here is a chart of some common subordinating conjunctions with examples of how to use them. Using these occasionally can help you diversify your sentence structure with complex sentences.

FUNCTION	SUBORDINATING CONJUNCTION	EXAMPLE
Concession	although, while, though, whereas, even though	Sarah completed her report even though she had to stay late to get it done.
Condition	if, unless, until	Until we know what is causing the problem, we will not be able to fix it.
Manner	as if, as, though	Everyone in the conference room stopped talking at once, as though they had been stunned into silence.
Place	where, wherever	Rita is in San Jose where she has several important client meetings.
Reason	because, since, so that, in order that	Because the air conditioning was turned up so high, everyone in the office wore sweaters.

Function	Subordinating Conjunction	Example
Time	after, before, while, once, when	After the meeting had finished, we all went to lunch.

As with conjunctive adverbs, when writing an essay or a report, don't use too many of these coordinators. The best kind of writing, whether it be academic or professional, is clear and concise. Therefore, only join two clauses that are logically connected and can work together to make one main point. If you repeat the same subordinating conjunction several times in a sentence, you are probably including more than one idea. This may make it difficult for readers to pick out the most important information in each sentence.

Sentence Combining: Run-on Sentences

Sentences with two or more independent clauses that have been incorrectly combined are known as **run-on sentences**. One way to correct run-on sentences is to correct the punctuation. For example, adding a period will correct the run-on by creating two separate sentences.

Run-on: There were no seats left, we had to stand in the back.
Corrected: There were no seats left. We had to stand in the back.

Using a semicolon between the two complete sentences will also correct the error. A semicolon allows you to keep the two closely related ideas together in one sentence. When you punctuate with a semicolon, make sure that both parts of the sentence are independent clauses.

Run-on: The accident closed both lanes of traffic we waited an hour for the wreckage to be cleared.
Complete sentence: The accident closed both lanes of traffic; we waited an hour for the wreckage to be cleared.

When you use a semicolon to separate two independent clauses, you may wish to add a transition word to show the connection between the two thoughts. After the semicolon, add the transition word and follow it with a comma.

Run-on: The project was put on hold we didn't have time to slow down, so we kept working.
Complete sentence: The project was put on hold; however, we didn't have time to slow down, so we kept working.

You can also fix run-on sentences by adding a comma and a coordinating conjunction. A coordinating conjunction acts as a link between two independent clauses. The acronym "FAN-BOYS" will help you remember this group of coordinating conjunctions. These are the seven coordinating conjunctions that you can use: "for," "and," "nor," "but," "or," "yet," and "so." Use these words appropriately when you want to link the two independent clauses.

> **Run-on:** The new printer was installed, no one knew how to use it.
> **Complete sentence:** The new printer was installed, but no one knew how to use it.

Adding **dependent words**, including subordinating conjunctions, is another way to link independent clauses. Like the coordinating conjunctions, dependent words show a relationship between two independent clauses.

> **Run-on:** We took the elevator, the others still got there before us.
> **Complete sentence:** Although we took the elevator, the others still got there before us.
> **Run-on:** Cobwebs covered the furniture, the room hadn't been used in years.
> **Complete sentence:** Cobwebs covered the furniture because the room hadn't been used in years.

Parallelism

Parallelism is the use of similar structure in related words, clauses, or phrases. It creates a sense of rhythm and balance within a sentence. Unbalanced sentences sound awkward and poorly constructed for readers. Read the following sentences aloud:

> **Faulty parallelism:** Kelly had to iron, do the washing, and shopping before her parents arrived.
> **Faulty parallelism:** Driving a car requires coordination, patience, and to have good eyesight.
> **Faulty parallelism:** Ali prefers jeans to wearing a suit.

All these sentences contain faulty parallelism. Although they are factually correct, the construction is clunky and confusing. In the first example, three different verb forms are used. In the second and third examples, the writer begins each sentence by using a noun ("coordination" and "jeans"), but ends with a phrase ("to have good eyesight" and "wearing a suit"). Now read the same three sentences that have correct parallelism.

Correct parallelism: Kelly had to do the ironing, washing, and shopping before her parents arrived.

Correct parallelism: Driving a car requires coordination, patience, and good eyesight.

Correct parallelism: Ali prefers wearing jeans to wearing a suit.

When these sentences are written using a parallel structure, they sound more aesthetically pleasing because they are balanced. Repetition of grammatical construction also minimizes the amount of work the reader has to do to decode the sentence. This enables the reader to focus on the main idea in the sentence and not on how the sentence is put together.

A simple way to check for parallelism in your writing is to make sure you have paired nouns with nouns, verbs with verbs, prepositional phrases with prepositional phrases, and so on. Underline each element in a sentence and check that the corresponding element uses the same grammatical form.

When you connect two clauses using a coordinating conjunction ("for," "and," "nor," "but," "or," "yet," "so"), make sure that the same grammatical structure is used on each side of the conjunction. Read the following example:

Faulty parallelism: When I walk the dog, I like to <u>listen to music</u> and <u>talking to friends</u> on the phone.

Correct parallelism: When I walk the dog, I like <u>listening to music</u> and <u>talking to friends</u> on the phone.

The first sentence uses two different verb forms ("to listen" and "talking"). In the second sentence, the grammatical construction on each side of the coordinating conjunction ("and") is the same, creating a parallel sentence.

The same technique should be used for joining items or lists in a series:

Faulty parallelism: This committee needs to decide whether the company should <u>reduce its workforce</u>, <u>cut its benefits</u>, or <u>lowering workers' wages</u>.

Correct parallelism: This committee needs to decide whether the company should <u>reduce its workforce</u>, <u>cut its benefits</u>, or <u>lower workers' wages</u>.

The first sentence contains two items that use the same verb construction ("reduce" and "cut)" and a third item that uses a different verb form ("lowering"). The second sentence uses the same verb construction in all three items, creating a parallel structure.

When you make a comparison, the two items being compared should have a parallel structure. Comparing two items without using parallel structure can lead to confusion about what is being compared. Comparisons frequently use the words "than" or "as," and the items on each side of these comparison words should be parallel. Read the following example:

Faulty parallelism: <u>Swimming in the ocean</u> is much tougher than <u>a pool</u>.
Correct parallelism: <u>Swimming in the ocean</u> is much tougher than <u>swimming in a pool</u>.

In the first sentence, the elements before the comparison word ("than") are not equal to the elements after the comparison word. It appears that the writer is comparing an action ("swimming") with a noun ("a pool"). In the second sentence, the writer uses the same grammatical construction to create a parallel structure. This clarifies that an action is being compared with another action.

To correct some instances of faulty parallelism, it may be necessary to add or delete words in a sentence.

Faulty parallelism: <u>A brisk walk</u> is as beneficial to your health as <u>going for a run</u>.
Correct parallelism: <u>Going for a brisk walk</u> is as beneficial to your health as <u>going for a run</u>.

In this example, it is necessary to add the verb phrase "going for" to the sentence to clarify that the act of walking is being compared to the act of running.

You can also fix faulty parallelism using **correlative conjunctions**. A correlative conjunction is a paired conjunction that connects two equal parts of a sentence and shows the relationship between them. Common correlative conjunctions include the following:

- either . . . or
- not only . . . but also
- neither . . . nor
- whether . . . or
- rather. . . than
- both . . . and

Correlative conjunctions should follow the same grammatical structure to create a parallel sentence. Read the following example:

Faulty parallelism: We can neither <u>wait</u> for something to happen nor <u>can we take</u> evasive action.
Correct parallelism: We can neither <u>wait</u> for something to happen nor <u>take</u> evasive action.

When using a correlative conjunction, the words, phrases, or clauses following each part should be parallel. In the first sentence, the construction of the second part of the sentence does not match the construction of the first part. In the second sentence, omitting needless words and matching verb constructions create a parallel structure. Sometimes, rearranging a sentence corrects faulty parallelism.

Faulty parallelism: It was both <u>a long movie</u> and <u>poorly written</u>.
Correct parallelism: The movie was both <u>long</u> and <u>poorly written</u>.

Note that the spelling and grammar checker on most word processors will not draw attention to faulty parallelism. When proofreading a document, read it aloud and listen for sentences that sound awkward or poorly phrased.

Good Paragraphs

Building a good paragraph is like building a good sandwich. Of course, you need good materials such as bread, meat, cheese, vegetables, and condiments. If you prefer a vegan example, it could be bread, peanut butter, and jelly. These are the individual ideas you write in your sentences. However, just having materials (ideas) isn't enough; they also have to be in the right order: a slice of bread, the first filling, the second filling, a slice of bread. Nobody would eat a sandwich that had jelly on the bottom, then peanut butter, then two slices of bread back-to-back with nothing between them. That paragraph would be a sticky mess. Arranging them in the correct order is important. Writing works the same way.

A strong paragraph contains three distinct components:

1. **Topic sentence:** The topic sentence is the main idea/argument of the paragraph.
2. **Body:** The body is composed of the **supporting sentences** that develop the main point.
3. **Conclusion:** The conclusion is the final sentence that summarizes the main point and perhaps **transitions** into the next paragraph.

The foundation of a good paragraph is the topic sentence, which expresses the main idea of the paragraph. The topic sentence relates to the **thesis**, or main point, of the essay and guides the reader by **signposting** what the paragraph is about. All the sentences in the rest of the paragraph should relate to the topic sentence. A paragraph should only have one main idea. That main idea is expressed in the topic sentence.

Topic Sentences

Pick up any newspaper or magazine and read the first sentence of an article. Do you have a good idea what the rest of the article is about? If so, you have likely read the topic sentence. An effective topic sentence combines a main idea with the writer's personal attitude or opinion. It serves to orient the reader and provides an indication of what will follow in the rest of the paragraph. Read the following example:

Topic sentence: Creating a national set of standards for math and English education will improve student learning in many states.

This topic sentence declares a favorable position for standardizing math and English education. After reading this sentence, a reader might reasonably expect the writer to provide supporting details and facts as to why standardizing math and English education might improve student learning in many states. If the purpose of the essay is to evaluate education in only one particular state, or to discuss math or English education specifically, then the topic sentence is misleading.

When writing a draft of an essay, ask a friend or classmate to read the opening line of your first paragraph. Ask your reader to predict what your paper will be about. If they are unable to guess your topic accurately, you should consider revising your topic sentence so that it clearly defines your purpose in writing.

There are five characteristics that define a good topic sentence:

1. A good topic sentence provides an accurate indication of what will follow in the rest of the paragraph.
2. A good topic sentence contains both a topic and a controlling idea or opinion.
3. A good topic sentence is clear and easy to follow.
4. A good topic sentence does not include supporting details.
5. A good topic sentence engages the reader by using interesting vocabulary.

Learning how to develop a good topic sentence is the first step toward writing a solid paragraph. Once you have composed your topic sentence, you have a guideline for the rest of the paragraph. To complete the paragraph, a writer must support the topic sentence with additional information and summarize the main point with a concluding sentence.

Supporting Sentences

Supporting sentences make up the body of the paragraph by explaining, proving, or enhancing the controlling idea in the topic sentence. Most paragraphs contain three to six supporting sentences depending on the audience and purpose for writing. A supporting sentence usually offers one of the following:

- Reason
  - o Example: The baby boomer generation's refusal to retire is contributing to the current lack of available jobs.
- Fact
  - o Example: Many families now rely on older relatives to support them financially.
- Statistics
  - o Example: Nearly 10% of adults are currently unemployed in the United States.

- Quotation
  - o Example: "We will not allow this situation to continue," stated Senator Johns.
- Personal Support
  - o Example: Last year, my uncle Bill was asked to retire at the age of fifty-five.

The type of supporting sentence you choose will depend on what you are writing and why you are writing. For example, if you are attempting to persuade your audience to take a position, you should rely on facts, statistics, and concrete examples rather than personal opinions. Read the following examples:

Topic sentence: There are numerous advantages to owning a hybrid car.

Supporting sentence (statistic): First, they get 20% to 35% more miles to the gallon than a fuel-efficient gas-powered vehicle.

Supporting sentence (fact): Second, they produce very few emissions during low speed city driving.
Supporting sentence (reason): Because they do not require gas, hybrid cars reduce dependency on fossil fuels, which helps lower prices at the pump.

Supporting sentence (personal example): Alexis bought a hybrid car two years ago and has been extremely impressed with its performance.

Supporting sentence (quotation): "It's the cheapest car I've ever had," she said. "The running costs are far lower than previous gas-powered vehicles I've owned."

Concluding sentence: Given the low running costs and environmental benefits of owning a hybrid car, it is likely that many more people will follow Alex's example soon.

The information you include in supporting sentences can come from a variety of sources, such as reference books, encyclopedias, websites, maps, dictionaries, newspapers, magazines, interviews, or your own previous experience or personal research.

Concluding Sentences

An effective concluding sentence draws together all the ideas you have raised in your paragraph. It reminds readers of the main point, the topic sentence, without restating it in the same words. Compare the topic sentence and concluding sentence from the previous example:

Topic sentence: There are numerous advantages to owning a hybrid car.
Concluding sentence: Given the low running costs and environmental benefits of owning a hybrid car, it is likely that many more people will follow Alex's example soon.

Notice the use of the **synonyms** "advantages" and "benefits." The concluding sentence reiterates the idea that owning a hybrid is advantageous without using the exact same words. It also summarizes two examples of the advantages covered in the supporting sentences: low running costs and environmental benefits.

You should avoid introducing any new ideas into your concluding sentence. A conclusion is intended to provide the reader with a sense of completion. Introducing a subject that is not covered in the paragraph will confuse the reader and weaken your writing.

A concluding sentence may do any of the following:

- Restate the main idea
  - o Example: Childhood obesity is a growing problem in the United States.
- Summarize the key points in the paragraph
  - o Example: A lack of healthy choices, poor parenting, and an addiction to video games are among the many factors contributing to childhood obesity.
- Draw a conclusion based on the information in the paragraph
  - o Example: These statistics indicate that unless we act, childhood obesity rates will continue to rise.
- Make a prediction, recommendation, or suggestion about the information in the paragraph
  - o Example: Based on this research, more than 60% of children in the United States will be morbidly obese by the year 2030 unless we take evasive action.
- Offer an additional observation about the controlling idea
  - o Childhood obesity is an entirely preventable tragedy.

Transitions

A strong paragraph moves seamlessly from the topic sentence into the supporting sentences and on to the concluding sentence. To help organize a paragraph and ensure that ideas logically connect to one another, writers use **transitional words and phrases**. A transition is a connecting word that describes a relationship between ideas. Take another look at the earlier example all put together with transitions words underlined:

There are numerous advantages to owning a hybrid car. First, they get 20% to 35% more miles to the gallon than a fuel-efficient gas-powered vehicle. Second, they produce very few emissions during low speed city driving. Because they do not require gas, hybrid cars reduce dependency on fossil fuels, which helps lower prices at the pump. Alexis bought a hybrid car two years ago and has been extremely impressed with its performance. "It's the cheapest car I've ever had," she said. "The running costs are far lower than previous gas-powered vehicles I've owned." All in all, given the low running costs and environmental benefits of owning a hybrid car, it is likely that many more people will follow Alexis' example soon.

Words such as "first" and "second" are transition words that show sequence or clarify order. They help organize the writer's ideas by showing that they have another point to make in support of the topic sentence. Other transition words that show order include "third," "also," and "furthermore."

The word "because" is a transition word of consequence that continues a line of thought. It indicates that the writer will provide an explanation of a result. In this sentence, the writer explains why hybrid cars will reduce dependency on fossil fuels ("because they do not require gas"). Other transition words of consequence include "as a result," "so that," "since," or "for this reason."

The following charts provide some useful transitions to connect supporting sentences and concluding sentences:

above all	but	for instance	in particular	moreover	on the contrary
also	conversely	furthermore	later on	nevertheless	subsequently
aside from	correspondingly	however	likewise	on the one hand*	therefore
at the same time	for example	in addition	meanwhile	on the other hand*	to begin with

For supporting sentences

*You can't use "on the other hand" unless you use "on the one hand" first. You can't have an "other" without a "first" hand. Use both to compare and contrast two things.

For Concluding Sentences

after all	all things considered	in brief	in summary	on the whole
all in all	finally	in conclusion	thus	to sum up

Academic Paragraphs

When reviewing directions for assignments, look for the verbs "summarize," "analyze," "synthesize," or "evaluate." Instructors often use these words to clearly indicate the assignment's purpose. These words will cue you on how to complete the assignment because you will know its exact purpose.

There are four common types of paragraphs you will write in academia:

Summary Paragraphs

- A summary shrinks a large amount of information into only the essentials. You probably summarize events, books, and movies daily. Think about the last movie you saw or the last novel you read. Chances are, at some point in a casual conversation with a friend, coworker, or classmate, you compressed all the action in a two-hour film or in a two-hundred-page book into a brief description of the major plot movements. While in conversation, you probably described the major highlights, or the main points, in just a few sentences using your own vocabulary and manner of speaking.
- Similarly, a summary paragraph condenses a long piece of writing into a smaller paragraph by taking out only the important information. A summary uses only the writer's own words. Like the summary's purpose in daily conversation, the purpose of an academic summary paragraph is to maintain all the essential information from a longer document. Although shorter than the original piece of writing, a summary should still communicate all the key points and key support. In other words, summary paragraphs should be clear and concise.

Analysis Paragraphs

- An analysis separates complex materials in their different parts and studies how the parts relate to one another. The analysis of simple table salt, for example, would require a deconstruction of its parts—the elements sodium (Na) and chlorine (Cl2). Then, scientists would study how the two elements interact to create the compound NaCl, or sodium chloride, which is also called simple table salt.
- Analysis is not limited to the sciences, of course. An analysis paragraph in academic writing fulfills the same purpose. Instead of deconstructing compounds, academic analysis paragraphs typically deconstruct documents. An analysis takes apart a primary source (an essay, a book, an article, etc.) point by point. It communicates the main points of the document by examining individual points and identifying how the points relate to one another.

Synthesis Paragraphs

- A synthesis combines two or more items to create an entirely new item. Consider the electronic musical instrument, the synthesizer. It looks like a simple keyboard but displays a dashboard of switches, buttons, and levers. With the flip of a few switches, a musician may combine the distinct sounds of a piano, a flute, or a guitar—or any other combination of instruments—to create a new sound. The purpose of the synthesizer is to blend the notes from individual instruments to form new, unique notes.

- The purpose of an academic synthesis is to blend individual documents into a new document. An academic synthesis paragraph considers the main points from one or more pieces of writing and links the main points together to create a new point, one not replicated in either document.

Evaluation Paragraphs

- An evaluation judges the value of something and determines its worth. Evaluations are done using standards, opinions, and prior knowledge. For example, at work, a supervisor may complete an employee evaluation by judging the worker's performance based on the company's goals. If the company focuses on improving the standard of communication, the supervisor will rate the employee's customer service according to a standard scale. However, the evaluation still depends on the supervisor's opinion and prior experience with the employee. The purpose of the evaluation is to determine how well the employee performs at their job.

- An academic evaluation shares your opinion and its reasons about a document or a topic of discussion. Evaluations are influenced by your reading of the document, your prior knowledge, and your experience with the topic or issue. Because an evaluation incorporates your point of view and reasons for your point of view, it typically requires more critical thinking and a combination of summary, analysis, and synthesis skills. Thus, evaluation paragraphs often come after summary, analysis, and synthesis paragraphs.

Thesis Statements

A **thesis statement** is one sentence, and it appears toward the end of your introduction paragraph. It is specific and focuses on one to three points of a single idea—points that can be demonstrated in the body. It forecasts the content of the essay and suggests how you will organize your information. Remember that a thesis statement does not summarize an issue but rather dissects it.

Do you know someone who isn't good at telling stories? You probably have trouble following their story as they jump from point to point, either being too brief in places that need explanation or providing too many details on a meaningless element. Maybe they tell the end of the story first, then move to the beginning, and later add details to the middle. Their ideas are scattered, and their stories don't flow well. When the story is over, you often have questions.

Just as a personal story can be a disorganized mess, an essay can be out of order and confusing. That is why writers need a thesis statement to provide a specific focus for their essay and to organize what they will discuss in the body.

Just like a topic sentence summarizes a single paragraph, the thesis statement summarizes an entire essay. It tells the reader the point you want to make in your essay, while the essay itself supports that point. It's like a signpost that signals the essay's destination. You should form your thesis before you begin to organize an essay, but it may need revision as the essay develops.

For every essay you write, you must focus on a central idea. This idea comes from a topic you have chosen or from a question your teacher has asked. It is not enough to just discuss a general topic or simply answer a question with a "yes" or "no." You have to form a specific opinion and then develop that into a controlling idea—the main idea upon which you build your thesis.

Remember that a thesis is not the topic itself, but rather your interpretation of the question or subject. For whatever topic your professor gives you, you must ask yourself, "What do I want to say about it?" Asking and then answering this question is vital to forming a thesis that is precise, forceful, and confident.

Thesis statements can be weak for several reasons, including:

- Simply stating your subject or a description of what your essay will discuss
  o Example: "My paper will explain why imagination is more important than knowledge."
- Making unreasonable or outrageous claims that insult the opposite side
  o Example: "Religious radicals across America are trying to legislate their puritanical beliefs by banning required high school books."
- Simply containing obvious facts that no one can disagree with
  o Example: "Advertising companies use sex to sell their products."
- Being too broad
  o Example: "The life of Abraham Lincoln was long and challenging."

A strong thesis statement needs to be specific, precise, arguable, demonstrable, forceful, and confident. Even in a personal essay that allows the use of first person, your thesis should not contain phrases such as "in my opinion" or "I believe." These statements reduce your credibility and weaken your argument. Your opinion is more convincing when you use a firm attitude.

Read the following examples of strong thesis statements:

- Closing all American borders for a period of five years is not a good solution to tackle illegal immigration.
- Compared to an absolute divorce, a no-fault divorce is less expensive, promotes fairer settlements, and reflects a more realistic view of the causes of marital breakdown.
- Exposing children from an early age to the dangers of drug abuse is a sure method of preventing future drug addictions.
- In today's crumbling job market, a high school diploma is not enough education to secure a stable, lucrative job.

Even after writing a "strong" thesis statement, you can still improve it by replacing non-specific words in your thesis, such as "people," "everything," "society," or "life," with more precise words to reduce vagueness.

You can find thesis statements in many places, such as in the news; in the opinions of friends, coworkers, or teachers; and even in songs you hear on the radio. Become aware of thesis statements in everyday life by paying attention to people's opinions and their reasons for those opinions. Pay attention to your own everyday thesis statements as well, as these can become material for future essays.

Audience

Focusing on your audience will improve your writing, even if the audience is clearly just your instructor. It can improve your writing because you will be thinking about what's inside their head as they read your writing. Specifically, what prior knowledge does your reader have, what expectations do they have while reading your writing, and what tone should you use to address that audience?

If your readers have studied certain topics, they may already know some terms and concepts related to the topic. You may decide whether to define terms and explain concepts based on your audience's prior knowledge. Although you cannot peer inside the brains of your readers to discover their knowledge, you can make reasonable assumptions. For instance, if your classmate who will read your paper is a nursing major, they will probably know more about health-related topics than a business major would.

As for their expectations, readers may expect consistencies in the assignment's appearance, such as correct grammar and traditional formatting like double-spaced lines and legible font. Readers may also have content-based expectations given the assignment's purpose and organization. In an essay titled "The Economics of Enlightenment: The Effects of Rising Tuition," for example, audience members may expect to read about the economic repercussions of college tuition costs. If your essay doesn't meet these language, formatting, and content expectations, they might become confused or upset or have some other negative reaction.

Finally, you should develop the right kind of tone for your specific audience. Tone identifies a speaker's attitude toward a subject or another person. You may notice a person's tone of voice easily in conversation. A friend who tells you about their weekend may speak excitedly about a fun skiing trip. An instructor may speak in a low, slow voice to emphasize their serious mood. Or, a coworker who is frustrated after a long meeting may make a sarcastic joke.

Just as speakers transmit emotion through voice, writers can transmit a range of attitudes through their writing, from excited and humorous to somber and critical. These emotions create connections among the audience, the author, and the subject, ultimately building a relationship between the audience and the text. To stimulate these connections, writers intimate their attitudes and feelings with useful devices, such as sentence structure, word choice, punctuation, and formal or informal language. Keep in mind that the writer's attitude should always appropriately match the audience and the purpose.

Introduction Paragraphs

An introduction serves the following purposes:

1. Attracts your reader with something intriguing
2. Establishes your voice, tone, and attitude toward the subject

3. Introduces the general topic of your essay
4. States the thesis that will be supported in the body paragraphs

First impressions are important and can leave lasting effects in your reader's mind. Therefore, the introduction is so important to your essay. If your introductory paragraph is boring or confusing, your reader probably will not have much interest in continuing with the essay.

Your introduction should begin with an engaging statement to provoke your readers' interest. In the next few sentences, introduce them to your topic by stating general facts or ideas about the subject. As you move deeper into your introduction, you gradually narrow the focus, moving closer to your thesis. Some call this the "funnel technique." You can visualize it in the following way:

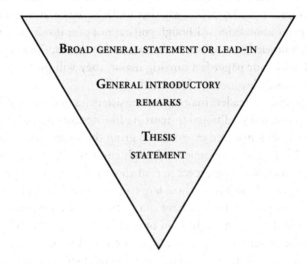

BROAD GENERAL STATEMENT OR LEAD-IN

GENERAL INTRODUCTORY
REMARKS

THESIS
STATEMENT

The "funnel technique," or moving from general to specific, is a very common introductory technique. Other good introductory "lead-in" techniques are the following:

- the use of a question (that is answered in the thesis)
- the use of a dictionary definition
- an anecdote (short personal story)
- background information (the "back story" that gives explanation as to why you are writing on this topic)
- a striking fact or statistic

Body Paragraphs

The body paragraphs present the evidence you have gathered to confirm your thesis. Before you begin to support your thesis in the body, you must find information from a variety of sources that support and give credit to what you are trying to prove.

Without primary support, your argument is not likely to be convincing. Primary support is the points you choose to expand on your thesis. It is the most important information you select to argue for your point of view. Each point you choose will be incorporated into the topic sentence for each body paragraph you write. Your primary supporting points are further supported by supporting details within the paragraphs.

To be good primary support, the information you choose must be specific, relevant, and detailed. Remind yourself of your main argument and delete any ideas that do not directly relate to it. Omitting unrelated ideas ensures that you will use only the most convincing information in your body paragraphs.

When you support your thesis, you are showing and explaining evidence. Evidence includes anything that can help support your stance. The following are the kinds of evidence you will encounter as you conduct your research:

- **Facts**: Facts are the best kind of evidence because they often cannot be disputed. They can support your stance by providing background information for your point of view. However, some facts may still need explanation. For example, the sentence "The most populated state in the United States is California" is a pure fact, but it may require some explanation to make it relevant to your specific argument.
- **Judgments**: Judgments are conclusions drawn from the given facts. Judgments are more credible than opinions because they are made through careful reasoning and examination of a topic.
- **Testimony**: Testimony is direct quotations from either a witness or an expert. A witness is someone who has direct experience with a subject; they add authenticity to an argument based on facts. An expert witness is a person who has extensive experience with a topic. This person studies the facts and provides commentary based on either facts or judgments, or both. An expert witness adds authority and credibility to an argument.
- **Personal observation**: Personal observation is like testimony, but personal observation consists of *your* testimony. It reflects what you know to be true because you have experiences and have formed either opinions or judgments about them. For instance, if you are one of five children and your thesis states that being part of a large family is beneficial to a child's social development, you could use your own experience to support your thesis. Be careful not to only use personal observation, however. Some readers may question your authority on a topic if you don't discuss any other people's testimony or provide any facts or judgments.

Each body paragraph contains a topic sentence that states one aspect of your thesis and then expands upon it. Like the thesis statement, each topic sentence should be specific and supported by concrete details, facts, or explanations. Topic sentences indicate the location and main points of the basic arguments of your essay. These sentences are important for writing your body paragraphs because they always refer to and support your thesis statement. Topic sentences are linked to the ideas you have introduced in your thesis, thus reminding readers what your essay is about. A paragraph without a clearly identified topic sentence may be unclear and messy, just like an essay without a thesis statement.

Conclusion Paragraphs

It's important to spend time writing your conclusion just like the rest of your essay. Too quick of an ending can ruin an otherwise strong essay. Similarly, a conclusion that does not correspond to the rest of your essay, has disconnected information, or is unorganized can unsettle your readers and raise doubts about the entire essay. However, if you have worked hard to write the introduction and body, your conclusion can often be the easiest part to compose.

A strong conclusion reviews your main points and emphasizes the importance of the topic. Many writers like to end their essays with a final emphatic statement. This strong closing statement will cause your readers to continue thinking about the implications of your essay; it will make your conclusion, and thus your essay, more memorable. Another powerful technique is to challenge your readers to make a change in either their thoughts or their actions. Challenging your readers to see the subject through new eyes is a powerful way to ease yourself and your readers out of the essay. Thinking about how your topic fits into the larger world view and expressing the wider, global issues is also another technique for the ending of your essay. Sometimes, this is called the "so, what?" conclusion (as in, why does this issue really matter? Or why is this important?).

Avoid doing the following things in your conclusion paragraph:

- **Introducing new material**: When you raise new points, you make your reader want more information, which you could not possibly provide in the limited space of your final paragraph.
- **Contradicting your thesis**: When you change sides or open your point of view in the conclusion, your reader becomes less inclined to believe your original argument.
- **Apologizing or using disclaimers**: Don't apologize for your opinion. Be strong and state what you think. Effective writers stand by their thesis statement.

When closing your essay, do not expressly state that you are drawing to a close. Your reader will know that a conclusion is forthcoming. In advanced academic writing, you would not necessarily rely on statements such as "in conclusion," "it is clear that," "as you can see," or "in summation." However, until you are more comfortable with essay writing skills, you should feel free to use a transition that indicates a closing.

20. ACADEMIC SITUATIONS AND SCRIPTS

People are not machines; there is no safe and accurate way to predict what someone will do or think when you say something to them. Sometimes, the message you send is not the same message that is received. Misunderstandings can happen, especially when you add culture to language and communication. If you have a loose script to help you structure an introduction for a conversation or an email, it might help you avoid uncomfortable or unpleasant communication. Please consider these academic situations below:

In Emails

EMAIL ADDRESSES

- Most professors and university staff members prefer that you use your official university email address when you email them. In fact, many universities require that all email communication must be through official school accounts. If you are not admitted to the school yet, then you will have to use your personal email account. However, after you are admitted, you should only use your official school account.
- If you don't already have one, I recommend creating a simple email address to use for academic and professional communication. Consider making a new account with a user name that is similar to your own name and that is easy to read.
- Do not email universities or professors from "unprofessional" or "unintelligible" personal email addresses. Your email address can affect how people judge you. For example, if your email address has words in it that are associated with violence and hate or with "unprofessional" topics such as sex and drugs, people may judge you negatively. Also, if your email is just a list of letters and numbers that don't mean anything, it will be hard for the recipient to remember your address.

SUBJECTS

- Write something meaningful in the "Subject" section of your email. Subject titles can be short and should not be complete sentences. Instead, include key words about the information contained in your email. Some professors or university staff members receive hundreds of emails every day. Therefore, a clear title will help them notice your email and help them respond appropriately. Good examples could include:
  o "Meeting Request for Tuesday"
  o "Question About Assignment #2"
  o "Sick, Will Miss Class Today"
  o "Check Out This YouTube Video!"
  o "EMERGENCY (PLEASE READ)"
- In the first three examples above, the subject title is short, easy to read, and contains hints about the information inside the email. Your professor can understand what you want and how important the email is just from the subject title. In the fourth example, the subject title says that you just want to share a resource and that it is probably not very important (or your professor can watch it after they respond to other emails). However, the last example stands out with capital letters and demands that your professor look at it immediately. Save subject titles like this for real emergencies.

SALUTATIONS

- Always begin emails with "Dear." Some people say this is outdated or not used often. However, it is safe and still considered proper for a formal email.
- After "Dear," use that instructor or person's preferred name and title. If you are not sure what they prefer or if you have not met them before, use their full public name (listed on a website, a business card, or on their office door label). Avoid gendered titles ("Dear Mr. X" or "Dear Ms. Y") unless you know that instructor's preference. Good examples could include:
  - "Dear Dr. X,"
  - "Dear Professor Y,"
  - "Dear Z," (if that instructor or person has told you to use their first name or a preferred name)
  - "Dear First Last," (where "First" is their given name and "Last" is their family name)
- After the body of your email, hit the enter key twice to create a blank line and then write a one-line "further action" sentence.
  - For example, if you are asking your professor a question in the body of the email, and if you need an answer to that question before the next class meeting, write a simple sentence such as: "Thank you, and I hope to hear from you before our next class meeting." This will be easy to see since you separated it from the body of your email, and it makes it clear for your professor what further action you are requesting of them.
  - Another example would be if you are sending information. After the body of your email, a simple sentence such as: "Thank you, and please let me know if you need anything else." This is inviting the receiver to contact you again. It is also a statement that you are not planning to send future information unless requested.
- At the end of your email, always sign off with a closing salutation. "Sincerely," and "Best wishes," are my favorites. Typically, I use "Best wishes," when the content of my email is positive and if I'm asking for information or a favor. I use "Sincerely," which really means "truthfully" or "honestly," when the content of my email is more serious or if I'm explaining and possibly apologizing for something.

FORMATTING

- Make your emails as clear and easy to read as possible. Take advantage of emphasis (bold, italics, underline), bullet points, numbered lists, and hyperlink functions when appropriate.
- Use **bolded text** when you want to make those words easy to see. For example: "Please come to **Room 509 by 14:00 on Tuesday** if you want to sign up for the party!"
- Use *italicized text* when you want to emphasize the tone or impact of a word or phrase in a sentence. For example: "I was *shocked and even frightened* by the comment my classmate made in our last class."
- Avoid using <u>underlined text</u> in emails. It is easy to confuse this for a hyperlink. The only time you should underline text is if your email is an announcement with a formal

title. That title should be centered in the email, should be a larger font size than the rest of your text, and then can also be underlined.

LENGTH

- In business, good emails are typically short because you just want to get information to someone quickly and clearly. Some business emails might leave salutations out and not even have full sentences written because the goal is to make the message short and less time-consuming. However, in academic emails, you should include salutations and write in complete sentences. Yes, it makes your emails longer, and it takes more time for you to write and more time for your reader to read. However, it shows more respect for the person you are sending the email to, and it gives you more of a chance to be clear with your statements/requests. Also, your professors are efficient readers. Therefore, as long as you format your email well, they should be able to skim through it quickly and get the information from it that they need.

FILE TYPES

- Whenever possible, email people files that are open-source or non-proprietary. For example, most of the time PC users cannot open files from Apple products such as Pages or Keynote. Similarly, people who do not have the Microsoft Office suite might not be able to open files such as Word (.docx), Publisher, or Access files. PDF files are typically safe for all operating systems.
- If a website or if an assignment's instructions clearly request a specific type of file, make sure you send that type.
- If you have enough time before that file is due to your receiver, you could send a simple email to ask: "Do you prefer any specific type of file?" or "Is it okay to send you a Keynote file?"

In the Classroom

Some students find jumping into classroom conversations difficult and intimidating. There are a few simple moves to help make this easier:

- If you are intimidated once a classroom conversation really get started, then try to be the first person to speak. As soon as the instructor offers up an open-ended question to the class for discussion, jump in! This might also be intimidating, but it can be much easier to be the first than to join in when a few students start dominating the speaking time.
- Raise your hand. Some professors will tell you that they don't want you to raise your hand or that they prefer if everyone just casually joins in a conversation. Even so, if you find it difficult or intimidating to speak while others are having a dialogue, raise your hand and keep it up until someone acknowledges you. Even if this is not your professor's preference, participating is better than not participating at all.
- Try to make connections with what other students have already said. You can agree with them, add something to what they said, disagree with them, or ask them (or the whole class) a follow-up question. When you do this, try to use their name as well.

This is a great way to make possible friends in the class, too. If you don't know their name, try to make eye contact with that person and point to them as you start speaking, and simply ask them for their name. After someone says something, you can raise your hand (or just speak if the class is that style) and say:

o   "I agree with what Shannon said about…"
o   "(Pointing at the person who spoke) Sorry, what was your name? (Person gives you their name). I want to agree with Ken's point about…"
o   "I like what Davina said about X, but I also think that…"
o   "I'm not sure about X, but I definitely think that Raul's point about Y is important because…"
o   "I have to disagree with—sorry, (pointing at the person who spoke) what was your name? (Person gives you their name). Yeah, Tina, I have to disagree because…"
o   "Paul, you said that X is important, but what about Y?"
o   "Sorry, (pointing at the person who spoke) what was your name? (Person gives you their name). Suzy, do you think your idea about X works for all the video clips we watched?"

In Office Hours

- Office hours are a great opportunity for you to speak with your instructor one-on-one. You can ask general questions about the course, you can clarify something the instructor said in class or wrote on their syllabus, you can go over an upcoming assignment's requirements and grading expectations, and sometimes you can ask them more mentorship questions such as benefits of majoring in their field, graduating from the university, and job opportunities after graduation. However, some students find that proximity intimidating and are unsure of how to start the conversation.

- Not all office hours look alike because not all offices look alike. Some professors have very nice, very welcoming, private office spaces where you can meet one-on-one (I had a spacious corner office with two windows at New Mexico Tech). Other professors share offices with another faculty member (as I do at Temple University, Japan Campus). If your instructor is a graduate student who teaches courses, they might share an office with many other graduate instructors (my office at the University of Connecticut held up to 6 instructors at once!). If your instructor is an adjunct, they might not even have a dedicated office on campus. You might meet with these instructors in a writing and learning center, in the school dining facilities, or outside on a walkway bench. Therefore, you will have to see how comfortable the environment is upon your arrival for office hours.

- Assuming your professor has their own private space, when you arrive, stand at the doorway and ask for permission to enter. Even if their office door is open, they might be busy working on something, and they might need just a few seconds to stop that action before you come in. As an academic coordinator, I often have sensitive information open on my computer such as student grades, and if a student suddenly comes in without asking for permission, it can be startling. Therefore, stand at the door, greet them, and simply say:

- o "Hi, Dr. Higgins, can I speak with you?"
- o "Excuse me, Dr. Higgins, can I come in?"
- o "Dr. Higgins, are you available now?"
- The magic recipe for a good office hours meeting includes:
  - o Come during the professor's scheduled office hours or during the time you previously arranged. Don't show up at their office at random times, and don't be late for scheduled appointments.
  - o Come with a specific goal in mind. Prepare your statement, prepare your question, and/or prepare a list of things you need from them.
  - o Bring in any work you have done.
  - o Come with a notebook or a device for taking notes. Take notes while they answer your questions. Show them that the office hour meeting was important and necessary.
  - o After your needs have been met, say "thank you" and leave. A bit of small talk and casual conversation is nice. However, be considerate of your professor's time and the time of your fellow students who might want to come to office hours after you. Don't use office hours as a simple way to "hang out" with your professor.

21. POP CULTURE INDEX

As an undergraduate English major, I was always looking for free books. Professors and graduate students at the University of California, Riverside filled bookshelves in the halls of the humanities building with outdated or unwanted books and journal issues. One of the titles that I noticed was Eric Donald Hirsch's *Cultural Literacy: What Every American Needs to Know* (1987). I was interested in both culture and literacy, and indeed, I was and still am an American. Therefore, I started looking through it to find out what I "needed to know." Inside, I found an appendix titled "The List," which included more than sixty pages of dates, names, subjects, and places, organized in two alphabetical columns. In order to be a "literate American," Hirsch thought I needed to know these things. These things included "the auricle" (a fancy word for "your ear"), "the cupola" (a rounded dome forming a ceiling), and a song titled "Home Sweet Home," which I assume is Henry Bishop's adaptation from John Howard Payne's 1823 American opera and not Mötley Crüe's 1985 glam metal song by the same title.

I felt offended. Who was this person to tell me what I "needed to know"? Who decides what information is important and what information is not? I know what Hirsch was trying to do—prepare people for the types of topics and questions that might come up in academic settings such as universities. However, I never heard anyone refer to any of these three things in all of my years of schooling, from my community college through my doctoral program. I *did*, however, hear people talk about Mötley Crüe, *Hamilton*, Clint Eastwood, *Slumdog Millionaire*, and many other popular culture references. Some of them I knew, but others I did not. It was these moments where I felt excluded that impacted me the most. Of course, some professors referred to obscure, archaic cultural artifacts, and they were *shocked* when their students were unfamiliar with that piece of high art. But I wasn't alone; many nineteen-year-old students in Southern California didn't know who André Breton was or what a theater proscenium is.

With this in mind, I have prepared lists of cultural references that I think will be much more useful for your actual college experience. Many of your professors will be between the ages of thirty and sixty. Some will be as young as twenty-two or twenty-three (master's or doctoral students who teach as graduate instructors or teaching assistants), and some will be in their seventies and above. They will all make references to the characters, histories, and symbols that mean the most to them, and they will hope that you understand what they are talking about. Great professors are often very aware of current events and trends as well because they are continually learning and seeking out new information. Therefore, the lists below primarily cover United States cultural references from the last twenty years. Every day on your commute to school on the bus/train or in your free time between classes, go on the internet and search for one or two of these figures. There is a good chance your university library will have audio and/or video recordings by these figures if you would like to check out their work. While you read about, listen to, or watch their performances, take some notes on this open textbook using a PDF program or in a physical journal.

I have included artists and works that have won awards simply because of the fame and notoriety that comes with winning awards. I am not saying these artists and works are necessarily any better than others. They are simply more talked about and more recognizable because of their award-winning status. I am also aware that many artists and works from historically underrepresented groups and backgrounds are correspondingly underrepresented here. Therefore,

I have tried to include lists of great films by African American, Asian American, and Hispanic and Latinx American directors.

Because people will often refer to these people and things by full name (such as "Philip Seymour Hoffman" instead of just "Hoffman"), these lists are organized alphabetically by first name.

Best African American Films

This list was published in the online version of Slate magazine on May 30, 2016, by Aisha Harris and Dan Kois. More than twenty prominent filmmakers, critics, and scholars chose these films directed by African Americans, ranging in release dates from 1920 through 2016. Notably, it does not contain more recent, widely appreciated films such as: *Black Panther* (2018), directed by Ryan Coogler; *BlacKkKlansman* (2018), directed by Spike Lee; *Get Out* (2017), directed by Jordan Peele; If Beale Street Could Talk (2018), directed by Barry Jenkins; *Moonlight* (2016), directed by Barry Jenkins; or *Straight Outta Compton* (2015), directed by F. Gary Gray.

12 Years a Slave (2013), directed by Steve McQueen
25th Hour (2002), directed by Spike Lee
Ashes and Embers (1982), directed by Haile Gerima
Belle (2014), directed by Amma Asante
Bessie (2015), directed by Dee Rees
Black Girl (1966), directed by Ousmane Sembène
Boyz n the Hood (1991), directed by John Singleton
Cooley High (1975), directed by Michael Schultz
Car Wash (1976), directed by Michael Schultz
Creed (2015), directed by Ryan Coogler
Crooklyn (1994), directed by Spike Lee
Daughters of the Dust (1991), directed by Julie Dash
Devil in a Blue Dress (1995), directed by Carl Franklin
Do the Right Thing (1989), directed by Spike Lee
Eve's Bayou (1997), directed by Kasi Lemmons
Friday (1995), directed by F. Gary Gray
Hollywood Shuffle (1987), directed by Robert Townsend
House Party (1990), directed by Reginald Hudlin
I Like It Like That (1994), directed by Darnell Martin
Juice (1992), directed by Ernest R. Dickerson
Just Another Girl on the I.R.T. (1992), directed by Leslie Harris
Killer of Sheep (1978), directed by Charles Burnett
Losing Ground (1982), directed by Kathleen Collins
Love and Basketball (2000), directed by Gina Prince-Bythewood
Malcolm X (1992), directed by Spike Lee
Medicine for Melancholy (2008), directed by Barry Jenkins
Middle of Nowhere (2012), directed by Ava DuVernay

Mo' Better Blues (1990), directed by Spike Lee
Night Catches Us (2010), directed by Tanya Hamilton
O.J.: Made in America (2016), directed by Ezra Edelman
Pariah (2011), directed by Dee Rees
Selma (2014), directed by Ava DuVernay
Sugar Cane Alley (1983), directed by Euzhan Palcy
Super Fly (1972), directed by Gordon Parks Jr.
Sweet Sweetback's Badasssss Song (1971), directed by Melvin Van Peebles
The Blood of Jesus (1941), directed by Spencer Williams
The Learning Tree (1969), directed by Gordon Parks
The Spook Who Sat by the Door (1973), directed by Ivan Dixon
The Watermelon Woman (1996), directed by Cheryl Dunye
Their Eyes Were Watching God (2005), directed by Darnell Martin
Timbuktu (2014), directed by Abderrahmane Sissako
To Sleep with Anger (1990), directed by Charles Burnett
Tongues Untied (1989), directed by Marlon Riggs
Touki Bouki (1973), directed by Djibril Diop Mambéty
Waiting to Exhale (1995), directed by Forest Whitaker
When the Levees Broke (2006), directed by Spike Lee

Best Asian American Films

This list was published in the online version of the *Los Angeles Times* on October 4, 2019, by Brian Hu. More than twenty Asian American critics and curators chose these films directed by Asian Americans, ranging from release dates in 2000 through 2019.

Advantageous (2015), directed by Jennifer Phang
American Revolutionary: The Evolution of Grace Lee Boggs (2013), directed by Grace Lee
Better Luck Tomorrow (2002), directed by Justin Lin
Colma: The Musical (2006), directed by Richard Wong
Columbus (2017), directed by Kogonada
Crazy Rich Asians (2018), directed by Jon M. Chu
Gook (2017), directed by Justin Chon
In Between Days (2006), directed by So Yong Kim
In the Family (2011), directed by Patrick Wang
Journey from the Fall (2006), directed by Ham Tran
Minding the Gap (2018), directed by Bing Liu
Refugee (2003), directed by Spencer Nakasako
Saving Face (2004), directed by Alice Wu
Searching (2018), directed by Aneesh Chaganty
Spa Night (2016), directed by Andrew Ahn
The Farewell (2019), directed by Lulu Wang
The Fast and the Furious: Tokyo Drift (2006), directed by Justin Lin

The Grace Lee Project (2005), directed by Grace Lee
The Motel (2005), directed by Michael Kang
The Namesake (2006), directed by Mira Nair

Best International Feature Film Winners

Before 2020, this category of the Academy Awards was called "Best Foreign Language Film." These films are produced outside the United States and use mostly non-English dialogue.

Year	U.S. Title	Original Title	Director(s)	Submitting Country	Language
2000	*Crouching Tiger, Hidden Dragon*	臥虎藏龍	Ang Lee	Taiwan	Mandarin
2001	*No Man's Land*	*Ničija zemlja*	Danis Tanović	Bosnia & Herzegovina	Bosnian, French, English
2001	*Nowhere in Africa*	*Nirgendwo in Afrika*	Caroline Link	Germany	German, English, Swahili
2003	*The Barbarian Invasions*	*Les Invasions barbares*	Denys Arcand	Canada	French
2004	*The Sea Inside*	*Mar adentro*	Alejandro Amenábar	Spain	Spanish
2005	*Tsotsi*	*Tsotsi*	Gavin Hood	South Africa	Zulu, Xhosa, Afrikaans
2006	*The Lives of Others*	*Das Leben der Anderen*	Florian Henckel von Donnersmarck	Germany	German
2007	*The Counterfeiters*	*Die Fälscher*	Stefan Ruzowitzky	Austria	German
2008	*Departures*	おくりびと	Yōjirō Takita	Japan	Japanese
2009	*The Secret in Their Eyes*	*El secreto de sus ojos*	Juan José Campanella	Argentina	Spanish
2010	*In a Better World*	*Hævnen*	Susanne Bier	Denmark	Danish
2011	*A Separation*	سیمین از نادر جدایی	Asghar Farhadi	Iran	Persian
2012	*Amour*	*Amour*	Michael Haneke	Austria	French
2013	*The Great Beauty*	*La grande bellezza*	Paolo Sorrentino	Italy	Italian
2013	*Ida*	*Ida*	Paweł Pawlikowski	Poland	Polish
2015	*Son of Saul*	*Saul fia*	László Nemes	Hungary	Hungarian
2016	*The Salesman*	فروشنده	Asghar Farhadi	Iran	Persian
2017	*A Fantastic Woman*	*Una mujer fantástica*	Sebastián Lelio	Chile	Spanish
2018	*Roma*	*Roma*	Alfonso Cuarón	Mexico	Spanish, Mixtec
2019	*Parasite*	기생충	Bong Joon-ho	South Korea	Korean, English

Best Hispanic and Latinx American Films

Some of the directors on this list do not hold United States citizenship nor do they call the United States home. However, since their films had a powerful impact on United States cinema history and popular culture, I included them on this list.

Amores Perros (2000), directed by Alejandro González Iñárritu
Frida (2002), directed by Julie Taymor and produced by Salma Hayek
Gravity (2013), directed by Alfonso Cuarón
Pan's Labyrinth (2006), directed by Guillermo del Toro
Selena (1997), directed by Gregory Nava
Roma (2018), directed by Alfonso Cuarón
Y Tu Mamá También (2001), directed by Alfonso Cuarón

The EGOT List

EGOT is an acronym that stands for Emmy, Grammy, Oscar, and Tony. People or productions on this list have won at least one of these awards in the last twenty years:

- Emmy Award (television) for "Best Comedy," "Best Drama," "Best Variety," "Lead Comedy Actor," "Lead Drama Actor," "Lead Comedy Actress," or "Lead Drama Actress"
- Grammy Award (music) for "Record of the Year," "Album of the Year," "Song of the Year," or "Best New Artist"
- Oscar, or the Academy Awards (film), for "Best Picture," "Best Actor," or "Best Actress"
- Tony Award (theater) for "Best Musical"

12 Years a Slave (film)
24 (television)
30 Rock (television)
A Beautiful Mind (film)
A Gentleman's Guide to Love and Murder (musical)
Adele
Adrien Brody
Alec Baldwin
Alison Krauss
Allison Janney
Ally McBeal (television)
America Ferrera
American Beauty (film)
Anderson .Paak
Arcade Fire
Argo (film)

Ariana Grande
Arrested Development (television)
Avenue Q (musical)
Beck
Ben Affleck
Bill Hader
Billie Eilish
Billy Elliott: The Musical (musical)
Billy Porter
Billy Ray Cyrus
Birdman or (The Unexpected Virtue of Ignorance) (film)
Black Panther (film)
Breaking Bad (television)
Brie Larson
Bruno Mars
Bryan Cranston
Cardi B
Casey Affleck
Cate Blanchett
Charlize Theron
Chicago (film)
Chick Corea
Claire Danes
Claire Foy
Game of Thrones (television)
Gary Oldman
Gladiator (film)
Glenn Close
Gloria Gaynor
Green Book (film)
Hadestown (musical)
Hairspray (musical)
Halle Berry
Hamilton (musical)
Helen Hunt
Helen Mirren
Herbie Hancock
Hilary Swank
Homeland (television)
In the Heights (musical)
James Gandolfini
James Spader
Jamie Foxx

Jean Dujardin
Jeff Bridges
Jeff Daniels
Jeffrey Tambor
Jennifer Aniston
Jennifer Lawrence
Jersey Boys (musical)
Jim Parsons
Joaquin Phoenix
Jodie Comer
John Cryer
John Lithgow
Jon Hamm
Julia Louis-Dreyfus
Julia Roberts
Julianna Margulies
Julianne Moore
Justice
Kacey Musgraves
Kate Winslet
Kelsey Grammer
Kevin Spacey
Kiefer Sutherland
Killing Eve (television)
Kinky Boots (musical)
Kirk Franklin
Kyle Chandler
Kyra Sedgwick
Lady Gaga
Last Week Tonight with John Oliver (television)
Late Show with David Letterman (television)
Lauryn Hill
Leonardo DiCaprio
Lil Nas X
Lizzo
Lost (television)
Mad Men (television)
Marion Cotillard
Mariska Hargitay
Matthew McConaughey
Matthew Rhys
Melissa McCarthy
Memphis (musical)

Meryl Streep
Michael Chiklis
Michael J. Fox
Million Dollar Baby (film)
Modern Family (television)
Moonlight (film)
Mumford & Sons
Natalie Portman
Nicole Kidman
Nipsey Hussle
No Country for Old Men (film)
Norah Jones
Olivia Colman
Once (musical)
OutKast
Parasite (film)
Patricia Arquette
Patricia Heaton
Philip Seymour Hoffman
Phoebe Waller-Bridge
Pose (television)
Rachel Brosnahan
Rami Malek
Ray Charles
Ray Romano
Reese Witherspoon
Renée Zellweger
Ricky Gervais
Robert Plant
Russell Crowe
Sally Field
Sandra Bullock
Santana
Sarah Jessica Parker
Sean Penn
Sela Ward
Sex and the City (television)
Slumdog Millionaire (film)
Spamalot (musical)
Spotlight (film)
Spring Awakening (musical)
Steely Dan
Sterling K. Brown

Tanya Tucker
Tatiana Maslany
Taylor Swift
The Artist (film)
The Band's Visit (musical)
The Book of Mormon (musical)
The Chemical Brothers
The Colbert Report (television)
The Daily Show with Jon Stewart (television)
The Departed (film)
The Handmaid's Tale (television)
The Hurt Locker (film)
The King's Speech (film)
The Lord of the Rings: The Return of the King (film)
The Marvelous Mrs. Maisel (television)
The Office (television)
The Practice (television)
The Producers (musical)
The Shape of Water (film)
The Sopranos (television)
The West Wing (television)
Thoroughly Modern Millie (musical)
Tina Fey
Toni Collette
Tony Shalhoub
Tyler, the Creator
U2
Vampire Weekend
Veep (television)
Viola Davis
Will & Grace (television)
Willie Nelson

The Literary List

People on this list are Americans (or people who spent a significant part of their writing careers in the United States) and have won the Nobel Prize for Literature (at any time), the Neustadt Prize, or the Pulitzer Prize for Fiction in the last twenty years.

Adam Johnson
Andrew Sean Greer
Anthony Doerr
Bob Dylan
Colson Whitehead

Cormac McCarthy
Donna Tartt
Edward P. Jones
Edwidge Danticat
Elizabeth Bishop
Ernest Hemingway
Eugene O'Neill
Geraldine Brooks
Isaac Bashevis Singer
Jeffrey Eugenides
Jennifer Egan
Jhumpa Lahiri
John Steinbeck
Joseph Brodsky
Junot Díaz
Michael Chabon
Michael Cunningham
Paul Harding
Pearl S. Buck
Raja Rao
Richard Powers
Richard Russo
Saul Bellow
Sinclair Lewis
Toni Morrison
Viet Thanh Nguyen

The Kennedy Center Honor List

People on this list have received a Kennedy Center Honor in the last twenty years for their contributions to American culture, regardless of their citizenship.

Andrew Lloyd Webber
Angela Lansbury
Al Green
Al Pacino
Barbara Cook
Barbra Streisand
Bill T. Jones
Billy Joel
Brian Wilson
Bruce Springsteen
Buddy Guy

Carmen de Lavallade
Carol Burnett
Carole King
Carlos Santana
Cher
Chita Rivera
Chuck Berry
Cicely Tyson
Clint Eastwood
Dave Brubeck
David Letterman
Diana Ross
Dolly Parton
Dustin Hoffman
The Eagles (Don Henley, Glenn Frey, Timothy B. Schmit, Joe Walsh)
Earth, Wind & Fire
Elizabeth Taylor
Elton John
George Jones
George Lucas
Gloria Estefan
Grace Bumbry
Hamilton: An American Musical creators (Lin-Manuel Miranda, Thomas Kail, Alex Lacamoire, and Andy Blankenbuehler)
Herbie Hancock
Itzhak Perlman
Jack Nicholson
James Brown
James Earl Jones
James Levine
James Taylor
Jerry Herman
Joan Sutherland
John Williams
Julie Andrews
Julie Harris
Led Zeppelin (John Paul Jones, Jimmy Page, and Robert Plant)
Leon Fleisher
Lily Tomlin
Lionel Richie
Linda Ronstadt
LL Cool J
Loretta Lynn

Luciano Pavarotti
Martha Argerich
Martin Scorsese
Martina Arroyo
Mavis Staples
Mel Brooks
Merle Haggard
Meryl Streep
Michael Tilson Thomas
Mike Nichols
Mikhail Baryshnikov
Morgan Freeman
Natalia Makarova
Neil Diamond
Oprah Winfrey
Ossie Davis
Patricia McBride
Paul McCartney
Paul Simon
Philip Glass
Plácido Domingo
Quincy Jones
Reba McEntire
Rita Moreno
Robert De Niro
Robert Redford
Ruby Dee
Sally Field
Seiji Ozawa
Sesame Street (television)
Shirley MacLaine
Smokey Robinson
Sonny Rollins
Steve Martin
Steven Spielberg
Sting
Suzanne Farrell
The Who (Pete Townshend and Roger Daltrey)
Tina Turner
Tom Hanks
Tony Bennett
Twyla Tharp
Van Cliburn

Warren Beatty
Wayne Shorter
Yo-Yo Ma
Zubin Mehta

The Kennedy Center Mark Twain Prize for American Humor

Named after the nineteenth century American humorist author, this prize is given to people who "had an impact on American society in ways similar to the distinguished 19th-century novelist and essayist Samuel Clemens, best known as Mark Twain." This often means that awardees have commented on society and social injustice in ways that make us laugh. The first award was given out in 1998.

~~Bill Cosby~~ (taken away in 2018 due to his sexual assault conviction)
Bill Murray
Billy Crystal
Bob Newhart
Carl Reiner
Carol Burnett
Dave Chappelle
Eddie Murphy
Ellen DeGeneres
George Carlin
Jay Leno
Jonathan Winters
Julia Louis-Dreyfus
Lily Tomlin
Neil Simon
Richard Pryor
Steve Martin
Tina Fey
Whoopi Goldberg
Will Ferrell

ABOUT THE AUTHOR

Shawn Higgins is a first-generation college graduate and first-generation graduate student from Ontario, California.

Shawn barely graduated high school. His father and his student record at Ontario High School in California can verify that. Shawn figured out in tenth grade that he could go to a community college after high school without focusing on getting high scores in school or on the SAT. Instead, he spent his time working part-time as a shop assistant at a fire suppression business, wrestling on his high school's team (losing most of the time), and singing and acting in his high school's choir and theater groups (doing pretty well at that, actually). Shawn's first dream out of high school was to be a musical theater director. Therefore, after (barely!) graduating high school, he enrolled at Riverside City College, which was locally well known for its theater classes and productions.

Shawn eventually graduated from Riverside City College with two associate degrees in arts and sciences. Simultaneously, he completed a one-year teaching certificate in TESOL (Teaching English to Speakers of Other Languages) from the neighboring University of California, Riverside Extension. Shawn's dream shifted from theater director to English professor. Shawn then transferred to the University of California, Riverside as a junior to major in American literature. Shawn earned his bachelor's degree in English (with high honors) and graduated with additional "university honors" after completing a senior thesis on Caribbean American literature.

Shawn then went to Columbia University in New York City for a master's in American Studies where he was a Dean's MA Scholarship recipient (one of only two in his department). At his first big academic conference, the Association for Asian American Studies' annual meeting of 2010 in Austin, Texas, he met Cathy J. Schlund-Vials from the University of Connecticut. She offered to become his mentor, and she took him on as a doctoral student in English at the University of Connecticut. In 2016, after defending his dissertation, titled

"Literary Soundscapes: Nationalism and U.S. Literature, 1890-1940," he secured his first full-time, tenure-track position as an assistant professor of English at the New Mexico Institute of Mining and Technology. At the end of his first year teaching there, he was honored with the 2017 Distinguished Teaching Award. In 2018, he left New Mexico Tech to become the academic coordinator for the Undergraduate Bridge Program at Temple University, Japan Campus in Tokyo.

In addition to his administrative interests, Shawn's research in American literature and trans-Pacific cultural studies has been published in various encyclopedias and in journals such as the Journal for Asian American Studies, Chinese America: History and Perspectives, China Review International, American Indian Quarterly, MusiCultures: Journal for the Canadian Society of Traditional Music, and Sounding Out! The Sound Studies Blog. Shawn has also served as a curriculum developer on the topics of resistance and social justice for The Fred T. Korematsu Institute.

Printed by Printforce, United Kingdom